Oshawa Ontario Book 2 in Colour Photos, Saving Our History One Photo at a Time

Photography by Barbara Raué
©2021

Series Name: Cruising Ontario

Book 205: Oshawa Book 2

Cover photo: 270 Simcoe Street North – Parkwood, McLaughlin Estate, Page 22

©2021 All the photos in this book have been taken with my cameras. I own the rights to them.

Series Name: Cruising Ontario
Saving Our History One Photo at a Time
in colour photos

Books Available in Alphabetical Order:
Aberfoyle, Acton, Ajax, Alton, Amherstburg, Ancaster, Arthur, Auburn, Aylmer, Ayr, Beaver Valley, Belgrave, Belleville, Bloomingdale, Blyth, Brantford, Brockville, Burford, Burlington, Caledon, Caledonia, Cambridge, Carlow, Chatsworth, Clifford, Collingwood, Conestogo, Delhi, Dorchester to Aylmer, Drayton, Drumbo, Dundas, Dunlop, Eden Mills, Elmira, Elora, Erin, Essex, Fergus, Goderich, Grimsby, Guelph, Hagersville, Hamilton, Hanover, Harriston, Hespeler, Jarvis, Kingston, Kingsville, Kitchener, Lake Superior, Lincoln, Linwood, Listowel, London, Lucknow, Merrickville, Mono, Mount Forest, Mount Pleasant, Neustadt, New Hamburg, Newboro, Newport, Niagara-on-the-Lake, Oakville, Onondaga, Orangeville, Orillia, Oshawa, Owen Sound, Palmerston, Paris, Pelham, Perth, Peterborough, Petrolia, Pickering, Port Colborne, Port Elgin, Portland, Preston, Rockwood, Sarnia, Sault Ste. Marie, Seaforth, Sheffield, Shelburne, Simcoe, Smiths Falls, Smithville, Southampton, St. Catharines, St. George, St. Jacobs, St. Marys, St. Thomas, Stoney Creek, Stratford, Thamesford, Thunder Bay, Tillsonburg, Toronto, Waterdown, Waterford, Waterloo, Welland, Wellesley, West Flamborough, Westport, Whitby, Windsor, Wingham, Woodstock

Book 200: West Flamborough
Book 201-202: Whitby
Book 203: Ajax and Pickering
Book 204-206: Oshawa

Table of Contents

Simcoe Street North					Page 6

Colborne Street West				Page 38

Colborne Street East				Page 45

Centre Street North					Page 46

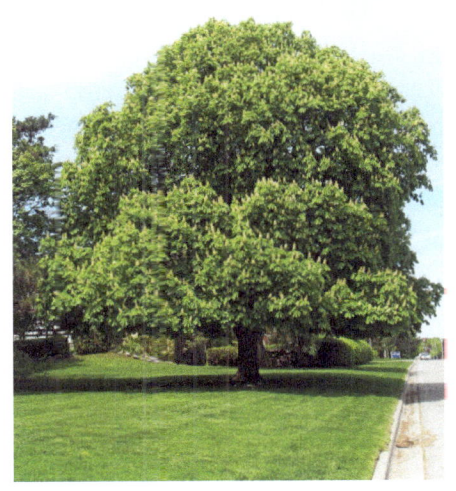

Oshawa is a city in Southern Ontario on the Lake Ontario shoreline. It is about sixty kilometres east of Downtown Toronto. The name Oshawa comes from the Ojibwa word meaning "the crossing place" or "where we must leave our canoes". More than 5,000 people work and more than 2,400 university students study in the downtown core.

Oshawa's roots are tied to the automobile industry with the Canadian division of General Motors located here. It was founded in 1876 as the McLaughlin Carriage Company. The lavish home of the carriage company's founder, Parkwood Estate, is a National Historic Site of Canada.

Historians believe that Oshawa began as a transfer point for the fur trade. Beaver and other animals trapped for their pelts by local natives were traded with the Coureurs des bois (voyagers). Furs were loaded onto canoes by the Mississauga Indians at the Oshawa harbor and transported to the trading posts located to the west at the mouth of the Credit River. Around 1760, the French constructed a trading post near the harbor location; this was abandoned after a few years, but its ruins provided shelter for the first residents of what later became Oshawa.

In the late eighteenth century a local resident, Roger Conant, started an export business shipping salmon to the United States. His success attracted further migration into the region. A large number of the founding immigrants were United Empire Loyalists, who left the United States to live under British rule. Later Irish and then French Canadian immigration increased as did industrialization. Oshawa and the surrounding Ontario County were the settling grounds of a large number of nineteenth century Cornish immigrants. The surveys ordered by Governor John Graves Simcoe, and subsequent land grants, helped populate the area. When Col. Asa Danforth laid out his York-to-Kingston road, it passed through the Oshawa area.

In 1822, a "colonization road" (a north-south road to facilitate settlement) known as Simcoe Street was constructed. It ran from the harbor to the area of Lake Scugog. It intersected the "Kingston Road: at what became Oshawa's "Four Corners."

In 1846 there were about 1,000 people in a community surrounded by farms. There were three churches, a post office, various types of tradesmen, a foundry, a grist mill and a fulling mill, a brewery, two distilleries, a machine shop and four cabinet makers.

The newly established village became an industrial center, and implement works, tanneries, asheries and wagon factories opened. In 1876, Robert Samuel McLaughlin, Sr. moved his carriage works to Oshawa from Enniskillen to take advantage of its harbor and of the availability of a rail link not too far away. He constructed a two-storey building, which was soon added to. This building was heavily remodeled in 1929, receiving a new facade and being extended to the north. Around 1890, the carriage works relocated from its Simcoe Street address to an unused furniture factory a couple of blocks to the northeast, and this remained its site until the building burnt in 1899. Offered assistance by the town, McLaughlin chose to stay in Oshawa, building a new factory across Mary Street from the old site. Rail service had been provided in 1890 by the Oshawa Railway; this was originally set up as a streetcar line, but by about 1910 a second freight line was built slightly to the east of Simcoe Street which provided streetcar and freight service, connected central Oshawa with the Grand Trunk (now Canadian National) Railway, and with the Canadian Northern (which ran through the very north of Oshawa) and the Canadian Pacific, built in 1912-13.

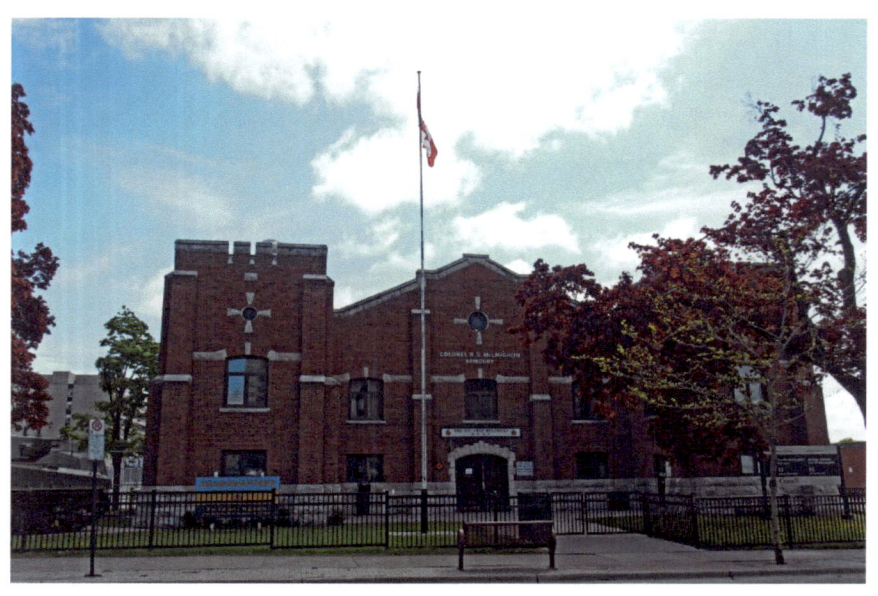

53 Simcoe Street North - Colonel R.S. McLaughlin Armoury - 1914

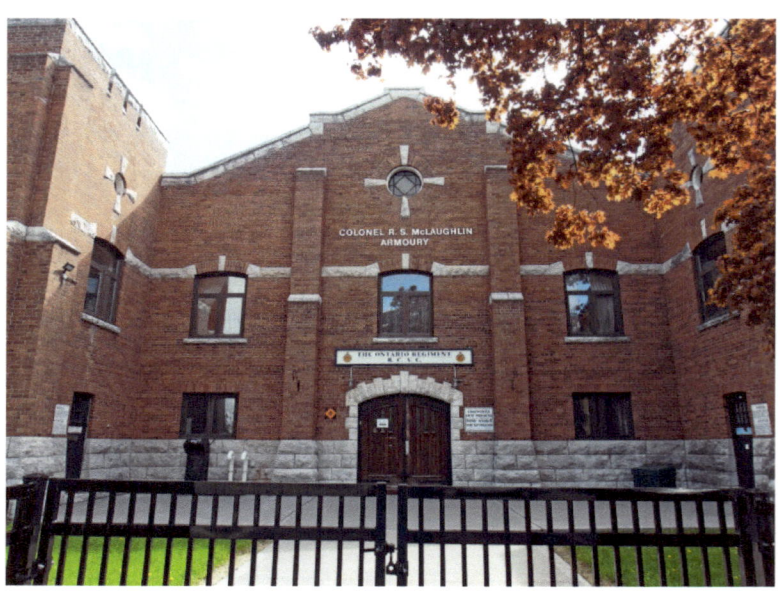

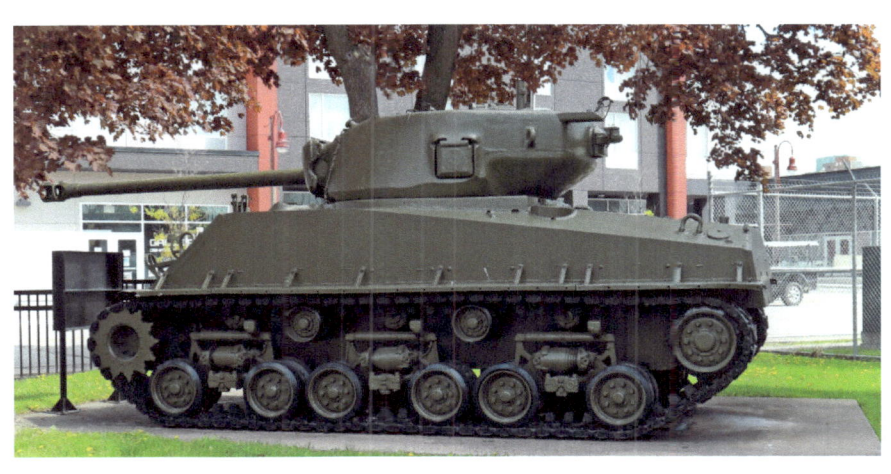

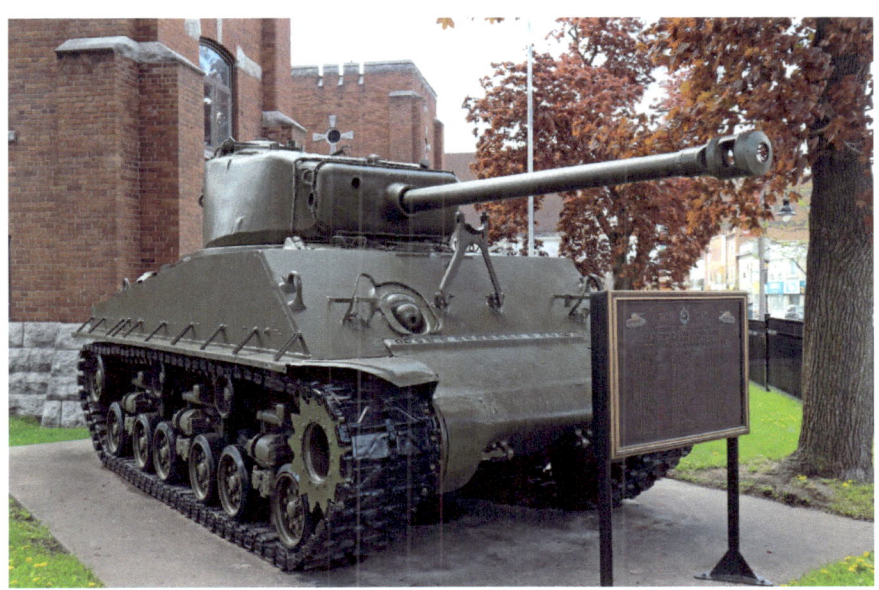

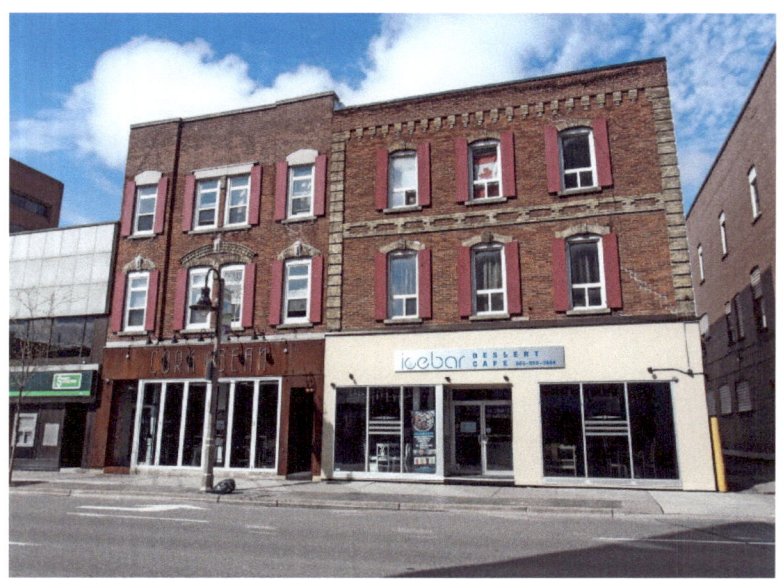

8 Simcoe Street North – 1860 - Murray Johnston's Store
10-14 Simcoe Street North - 1881

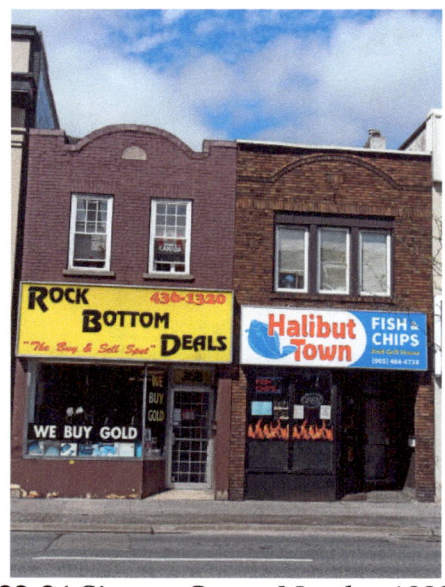

22-24 Simcoe Street North - 1923

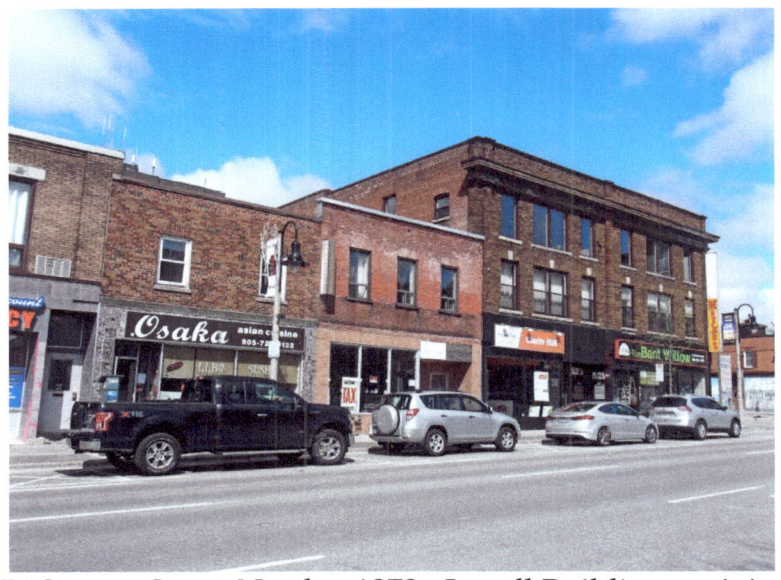

46-54 Simcoe Street North – 1878 - Lovell Building - originally McLaughlin Carriage Company (50-54)

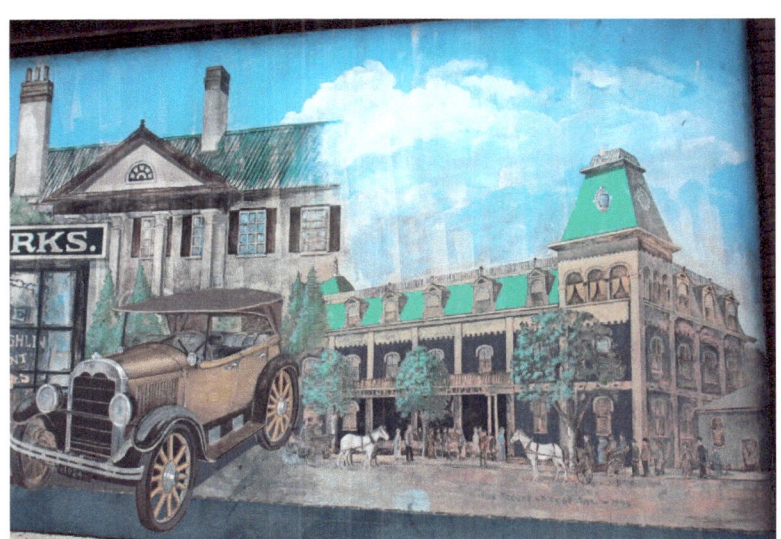

"Full Steam Ahead" Mural by Gus Froese – Queen's Hotel established in 1874

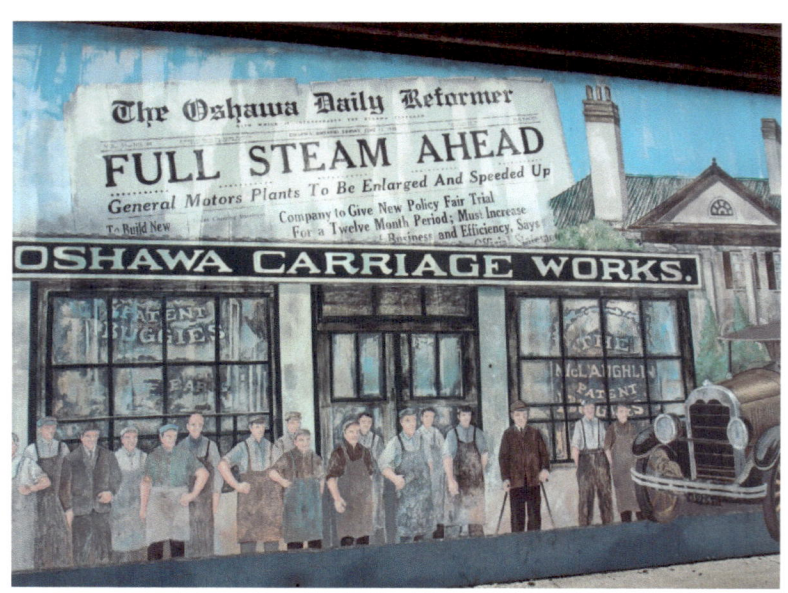

Mural – Oshawa Carriage Works

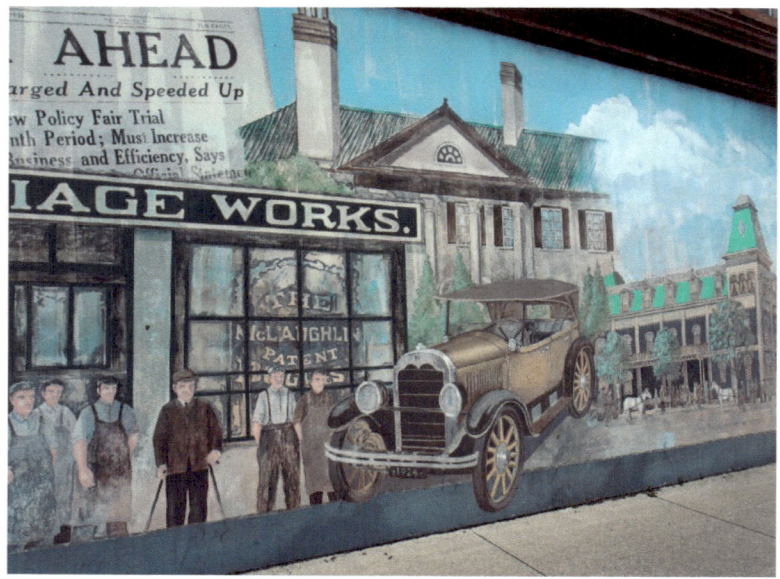

1924 McLaughlin Buick

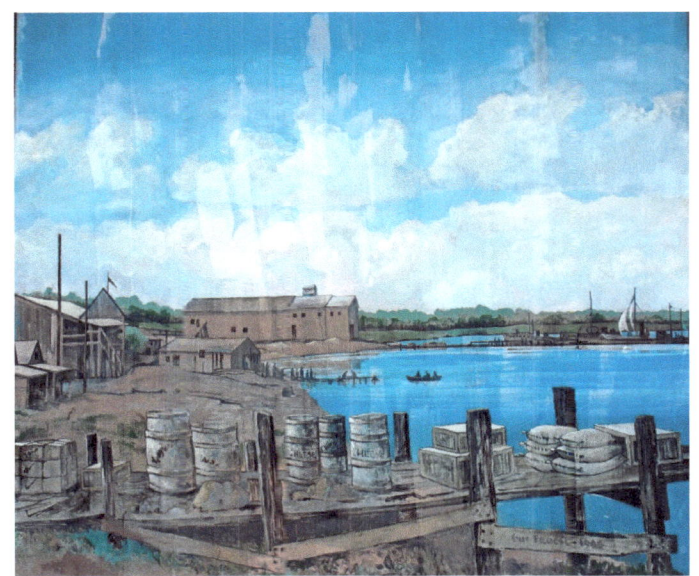

Mural – Sydenham Harbor

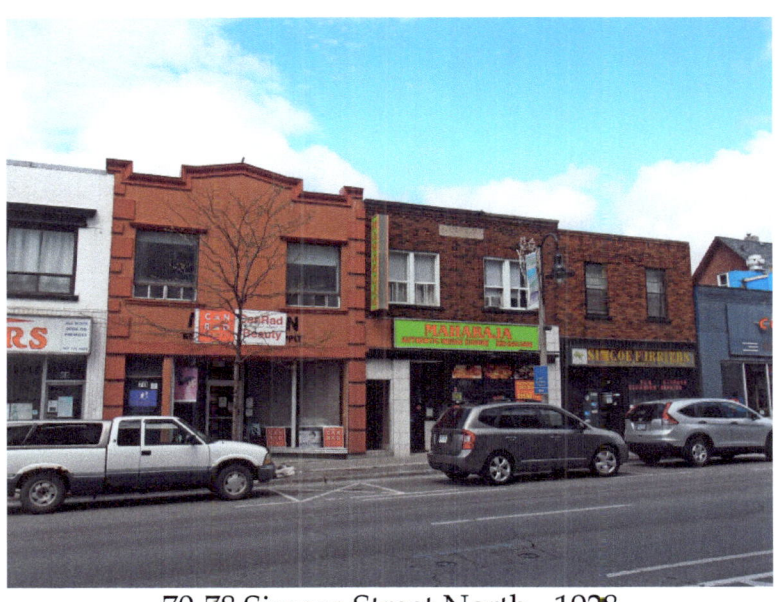

70-78 Simcoe Street North - 1928

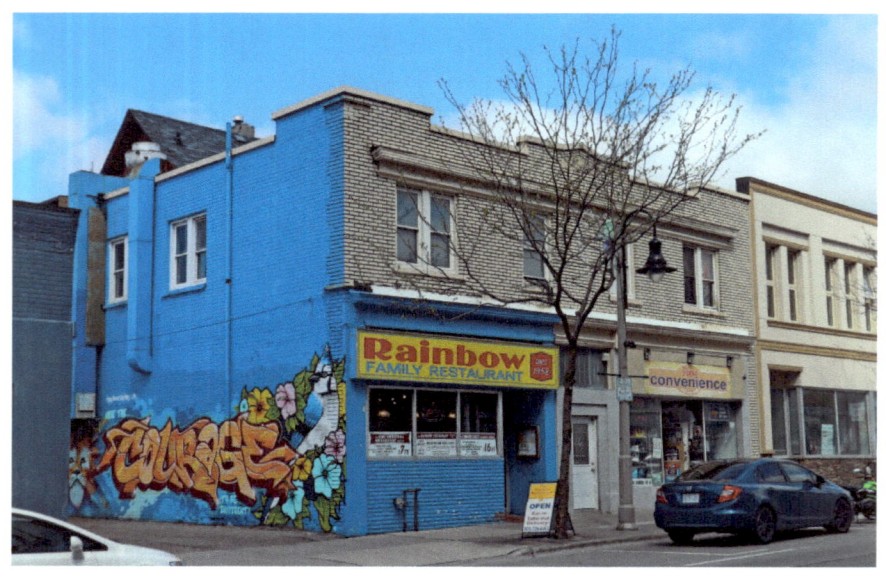

86 Simcoe Street North – Jones Block – 1927 – stepped parapet

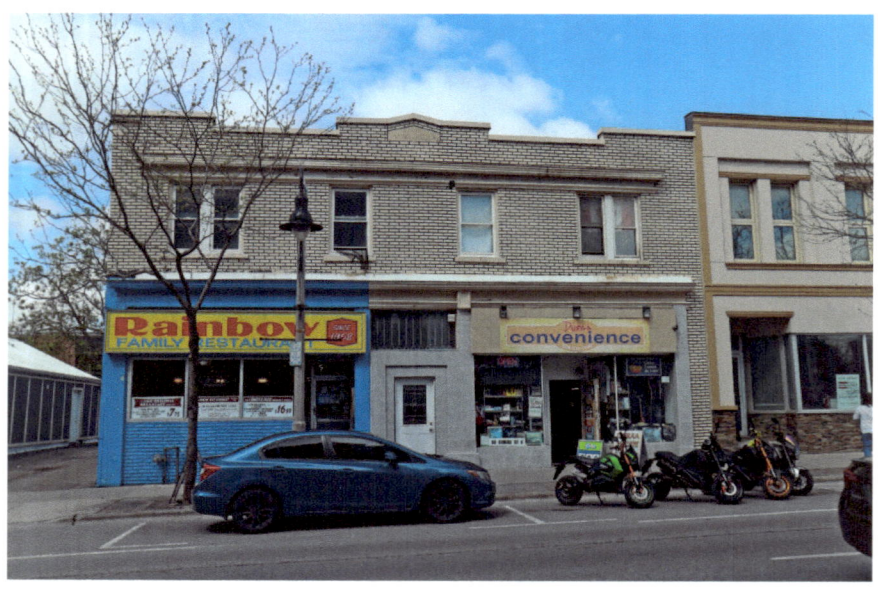

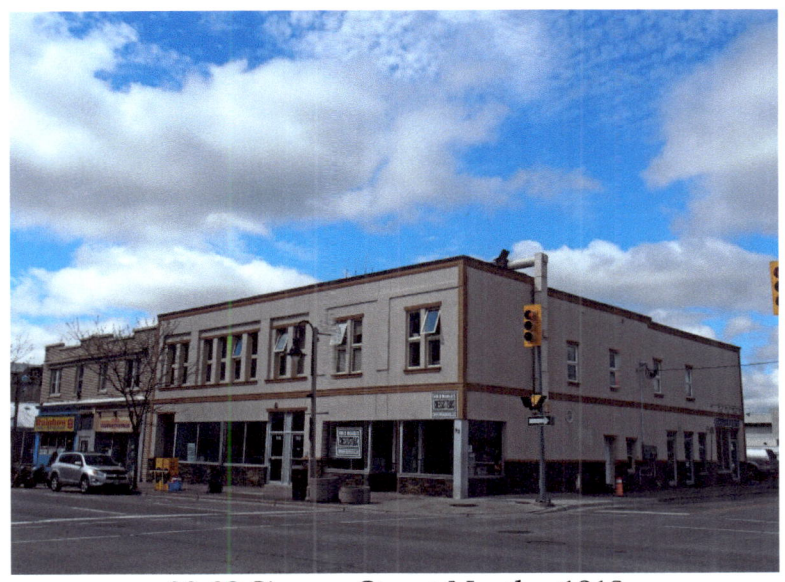

90-92 Simcoe Street North - 1918

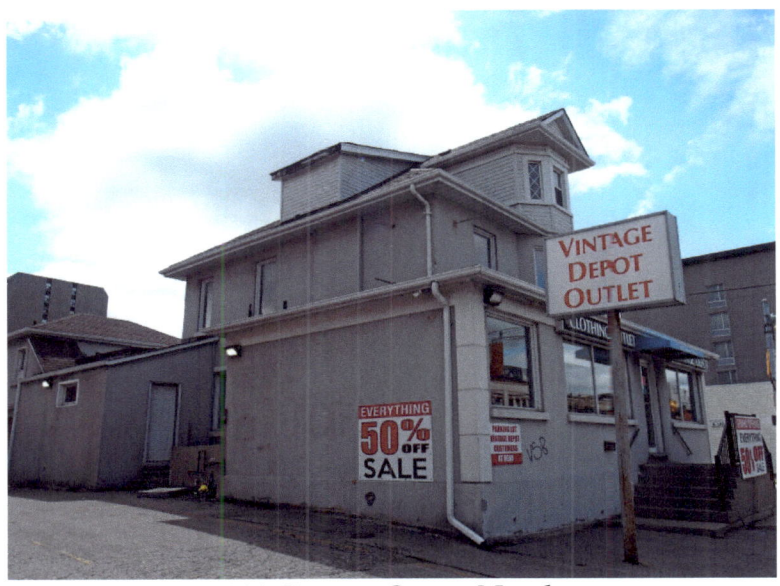

101 Simcoe Street North

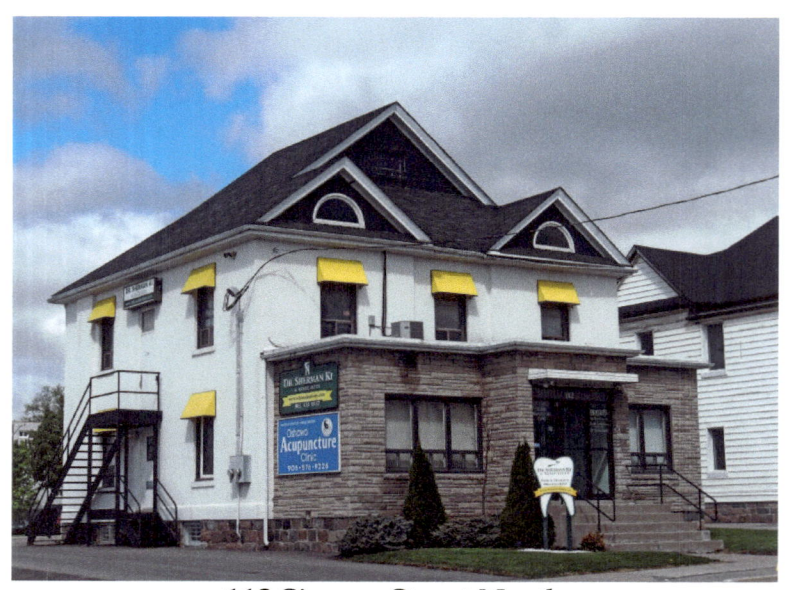

112 Simcoe Street North

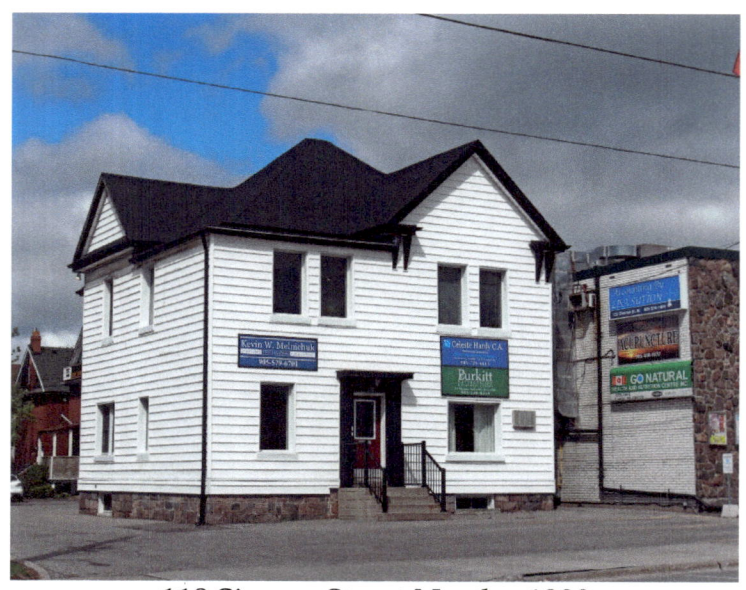

118 Simcoe Street North - 1900

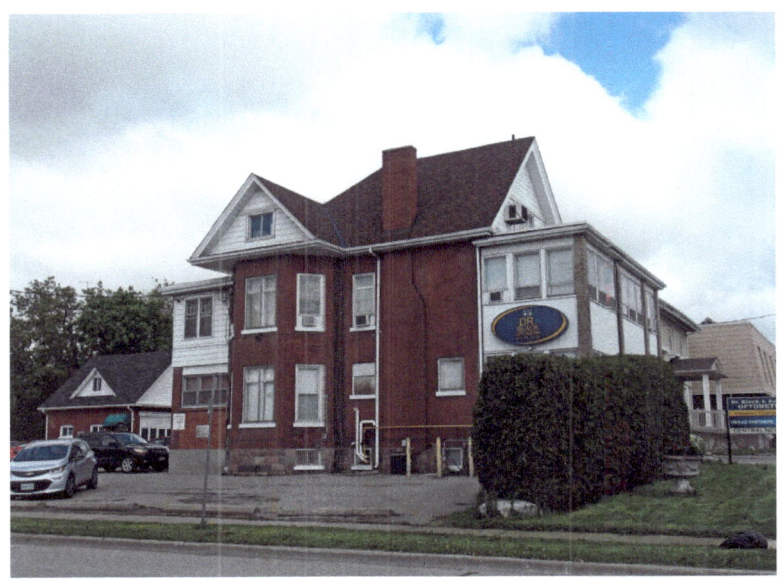

136 Simcoe Street North

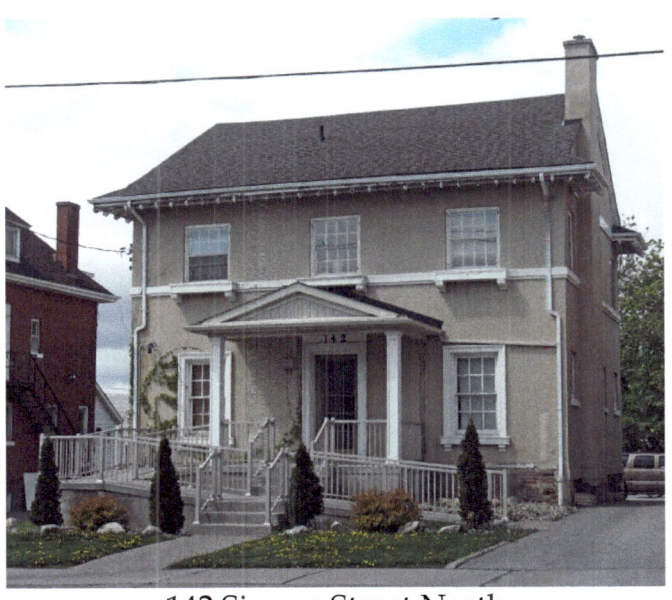

142 Simcoe Street North

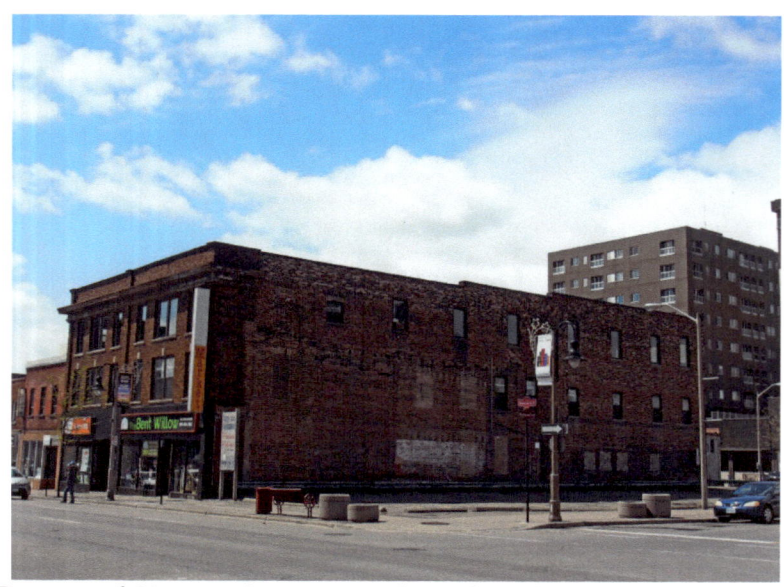

Corner of Simcoe Street North and Richmond Street West

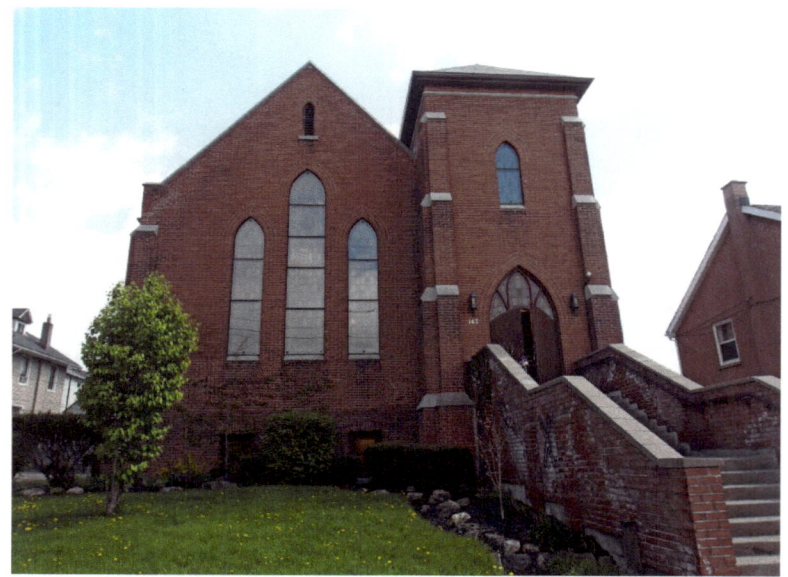

147 Simcoe Street North – Knox Presbyterian Church – 1934 - C.C. Stenhouse - architect

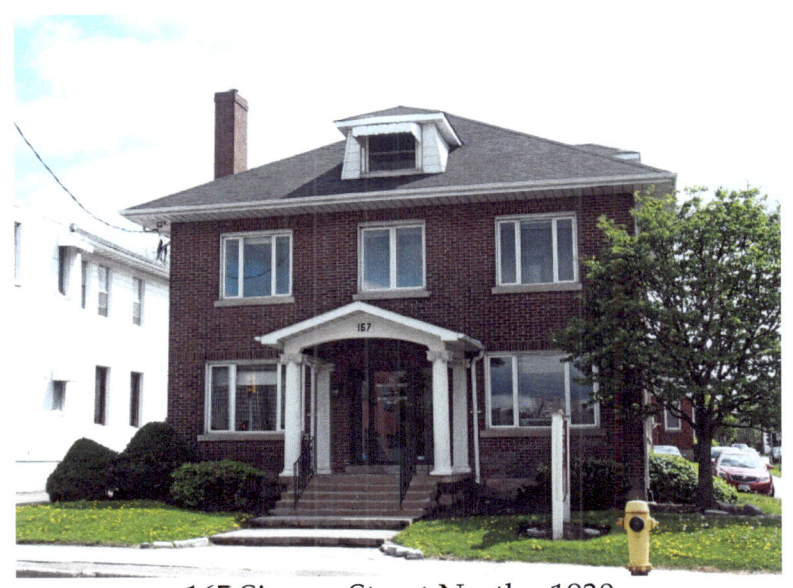

167 Simcoe Street North - 1930

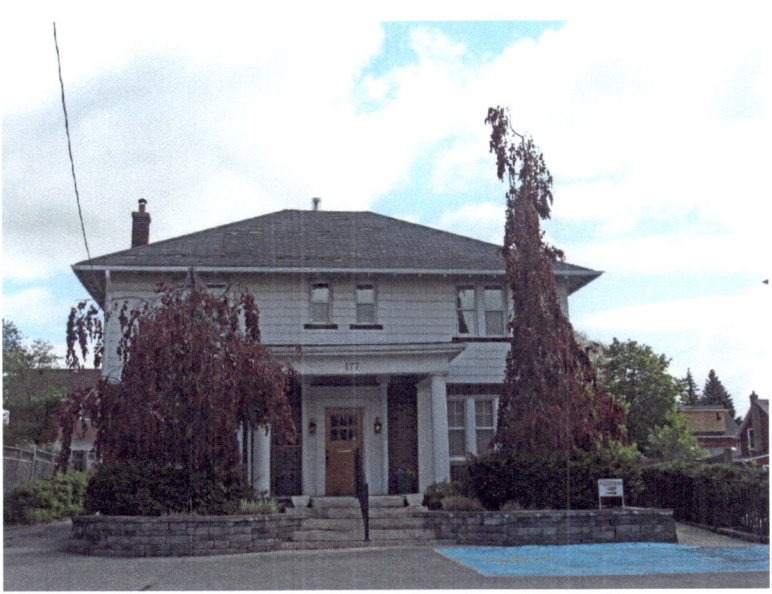

177 Simcoe Street North - 1925

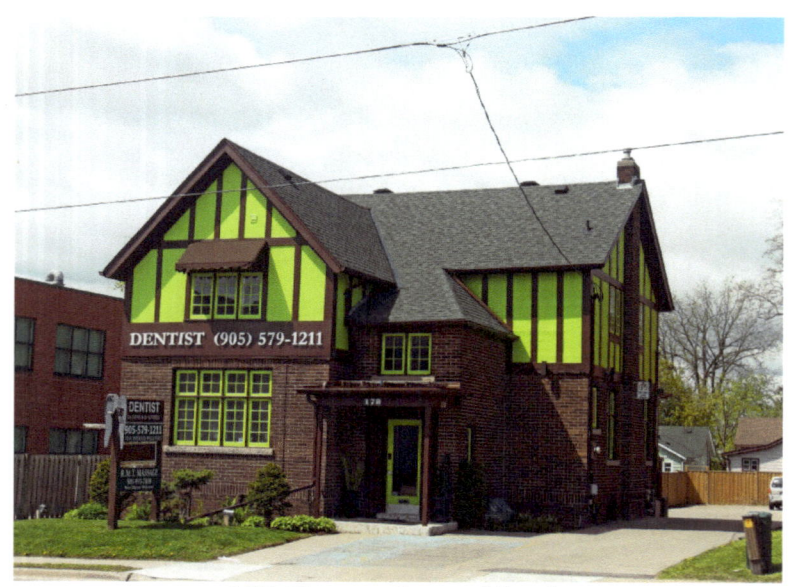

178 Simcoe Street North

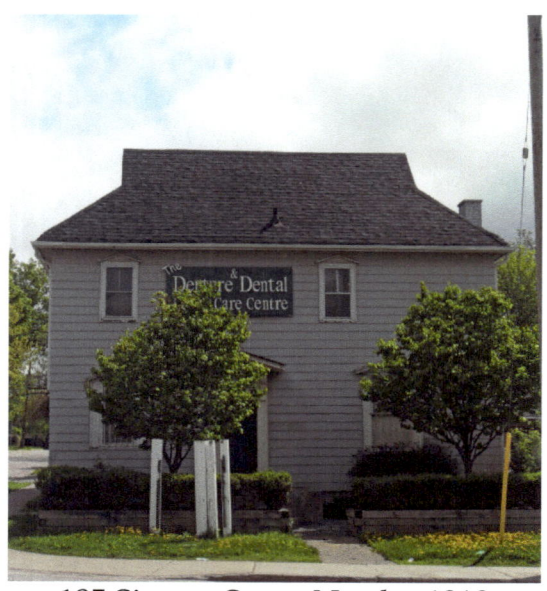

185 Simcoe Street North - 1910

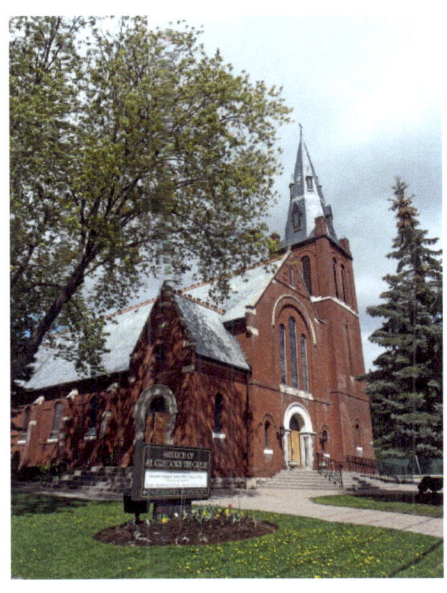

194 Simcoe Street North – St. Gregory's Catholic Church - 1892

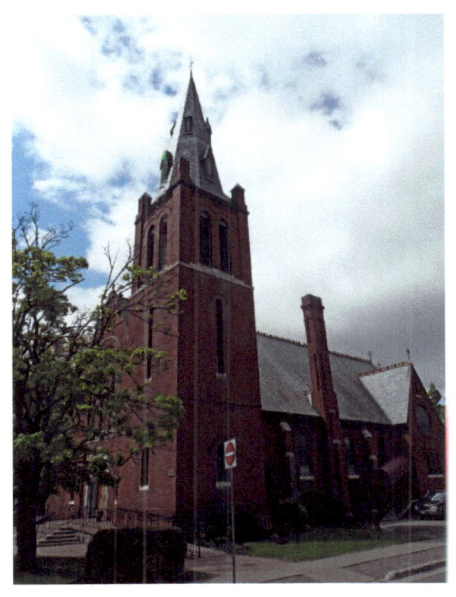

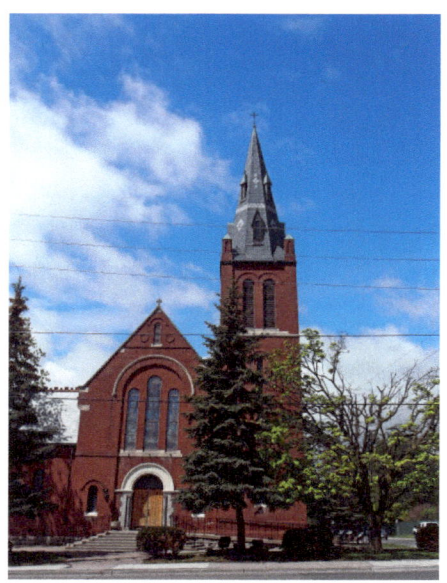
194 Simcoe Street North

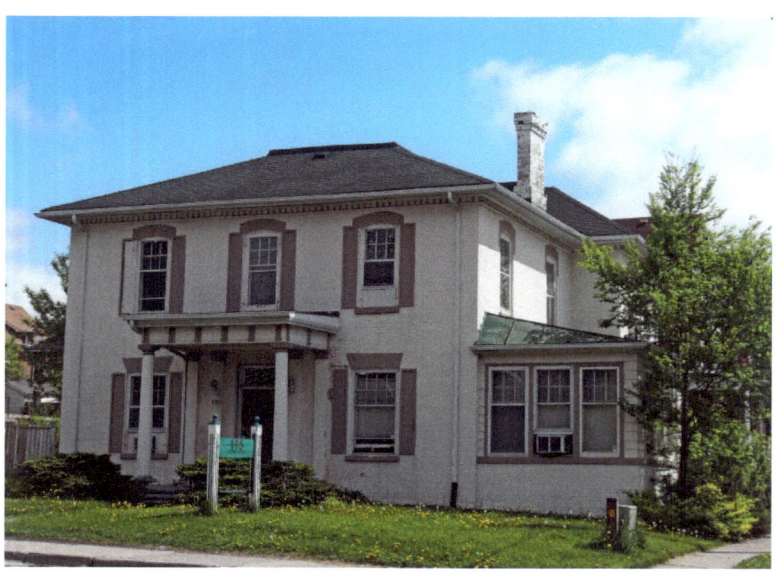
195 Simcoe Street North - R.S McLaughlin Home - 1887

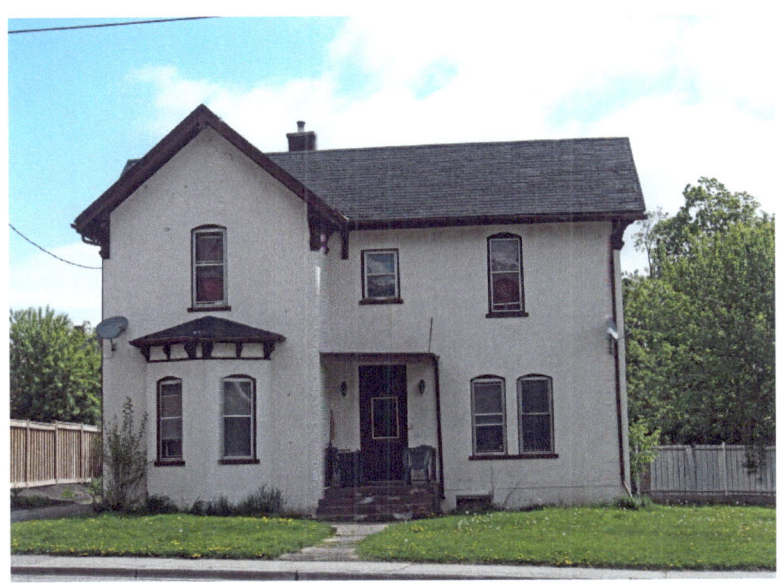
202 Simcoe Street North - 1890

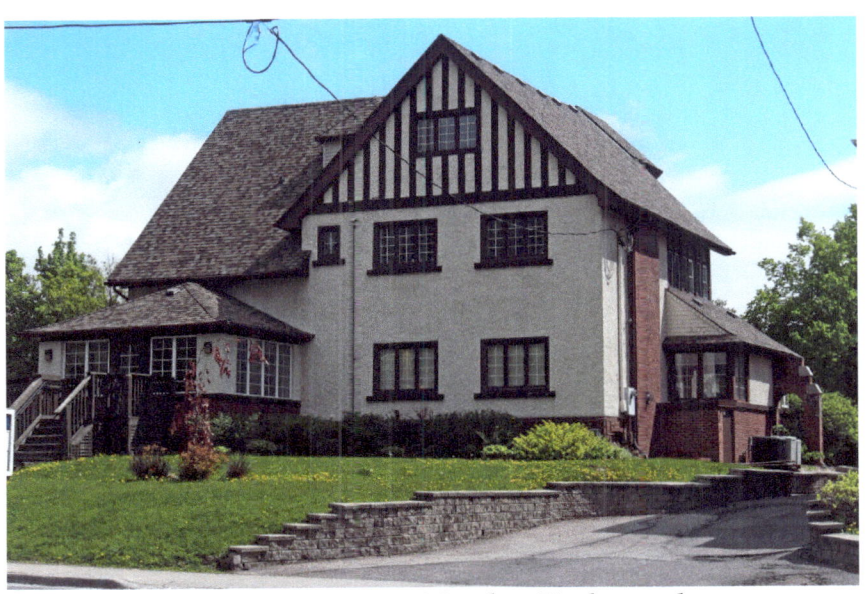
213 Simcoe Street North – Tudor style

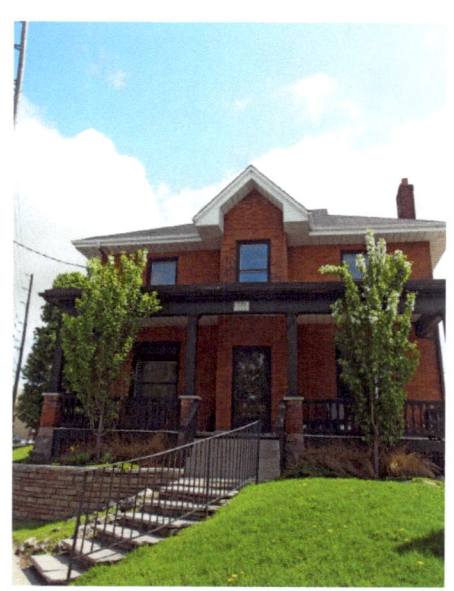

231 Simcoe Street North

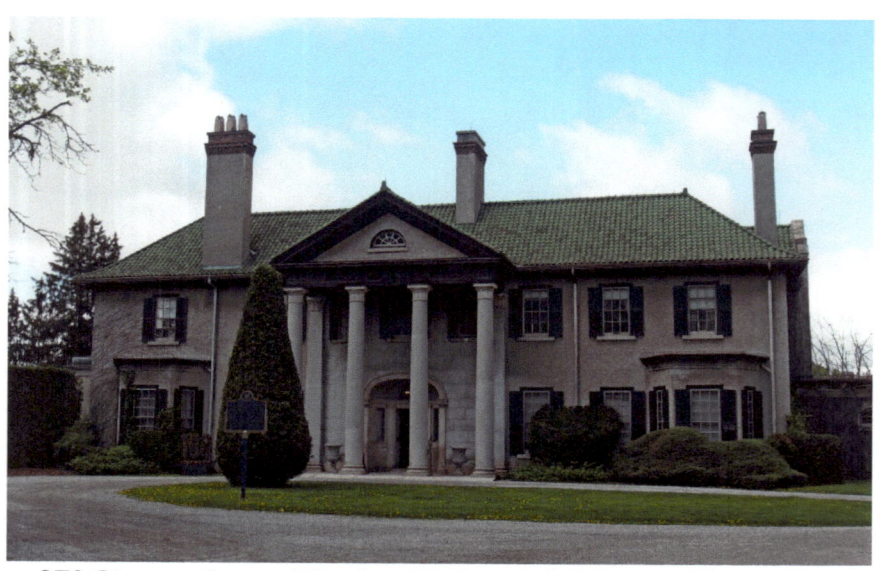

270 Simcoe Street North – Parkwood, McLaughlin Estate

Colonel Robert Samuel McLaughlin and "Billy" Durant signed a 15-year contract in 1907, under which the McLaughlin Motor Company began to manufacture automobiles under the McLaughlin name, using Buick engines and other mechanical parts. Buick was merged into General Motors shortly after, and in 1915 the firm acquired the manufacturing rights to the Chevrolet brand. Within three years, the McLaughlin Motor Car Company and the Chevrolet Motor Car Company of Canada merged, creating General Motors of Canada in 1918 with McLaughlin as President.

With the wealth he gained in his business venture, in 1916 McLaughlin built one of the most stately homes in Canada, "Parkwood". The 55-room residence was designed by Toronto architect John M. Lyle. McLaughlin lived in the house for 55 years with his wife and they raised five daughters. The house replaced an older mansion, which was about 30 years old when it was demolished; the grounds of the earlier home had been operated as Prospect Park, and this land was acquired by the town and became its first municipal park, Alexandra Park. Parkwood today is open to the public as a National Historic Site.

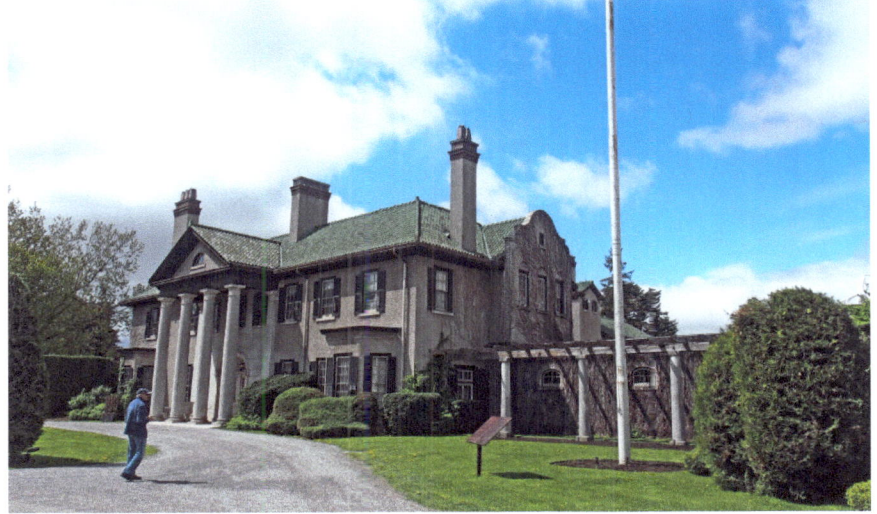

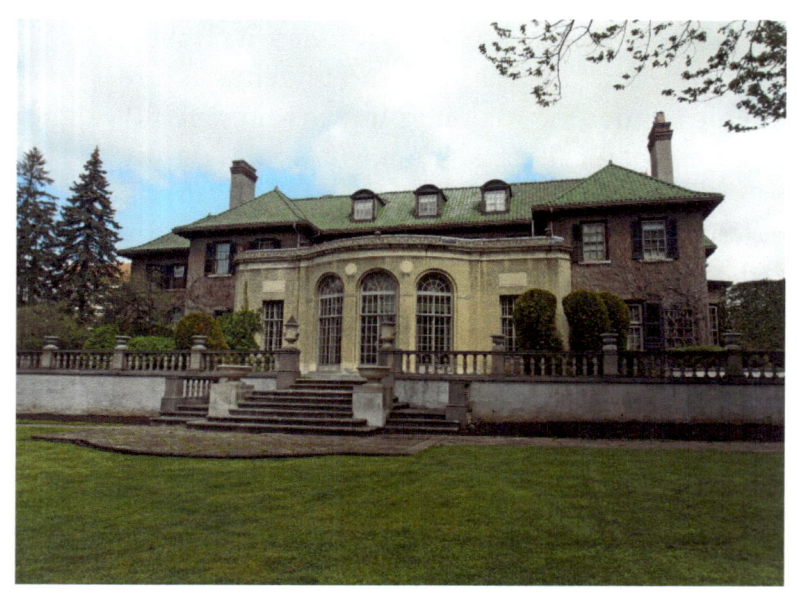

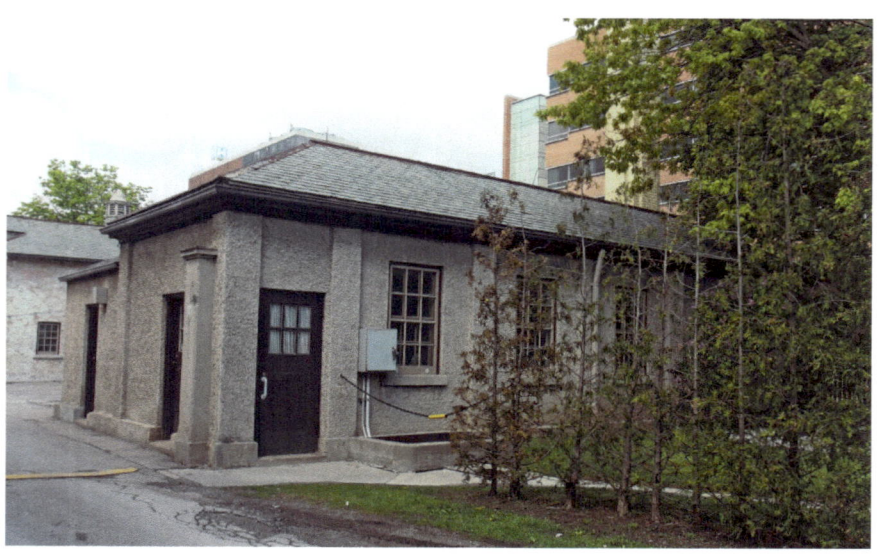

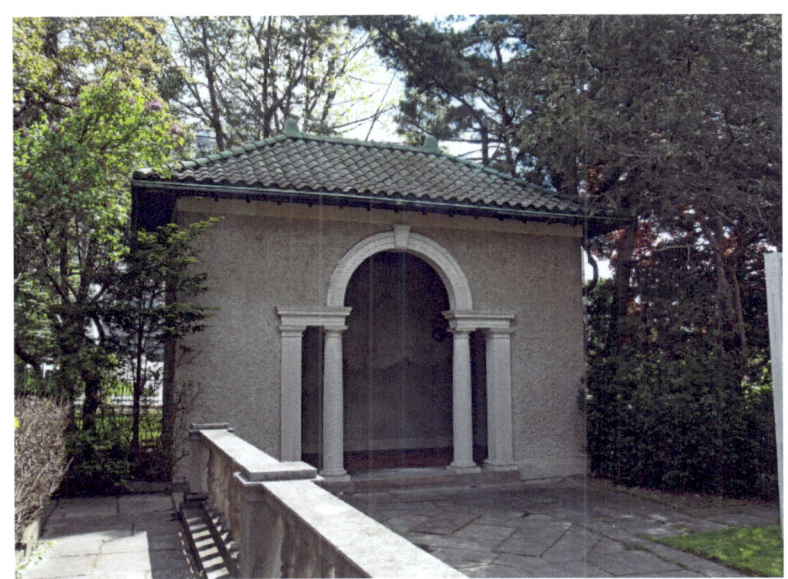

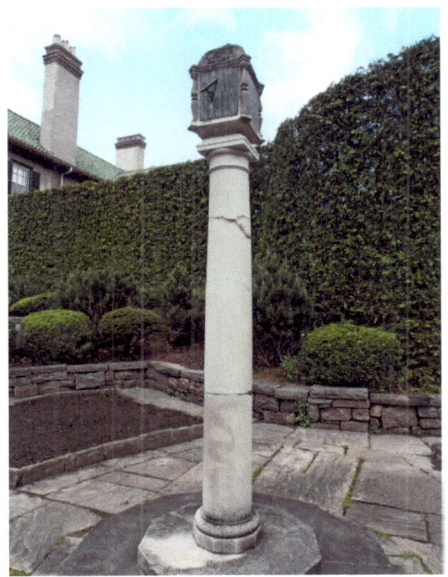

Sundial – "Let others tell of storms and showers; I'll only count your sunny hours. Let the slight shadow teach thee wisdom. Amyddst ye fflowers I tell thee houres."

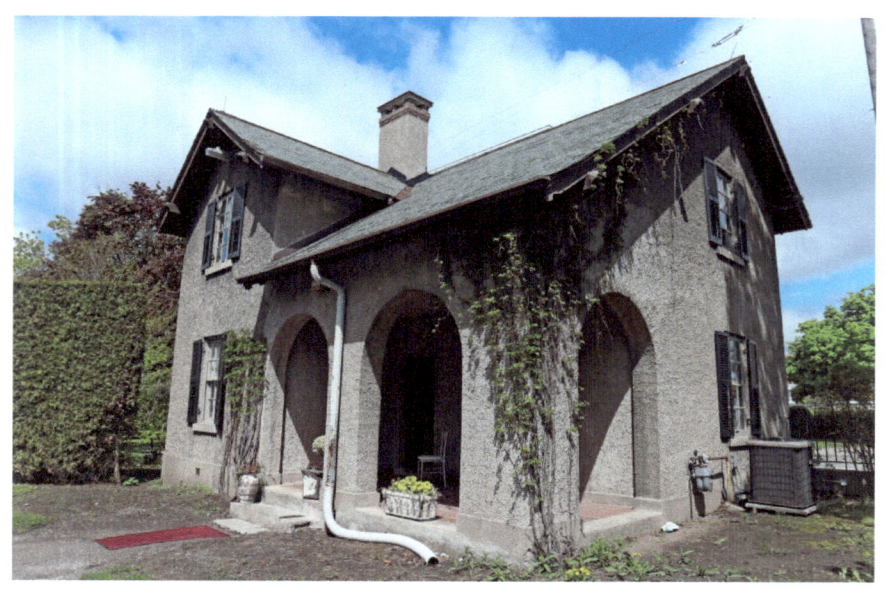

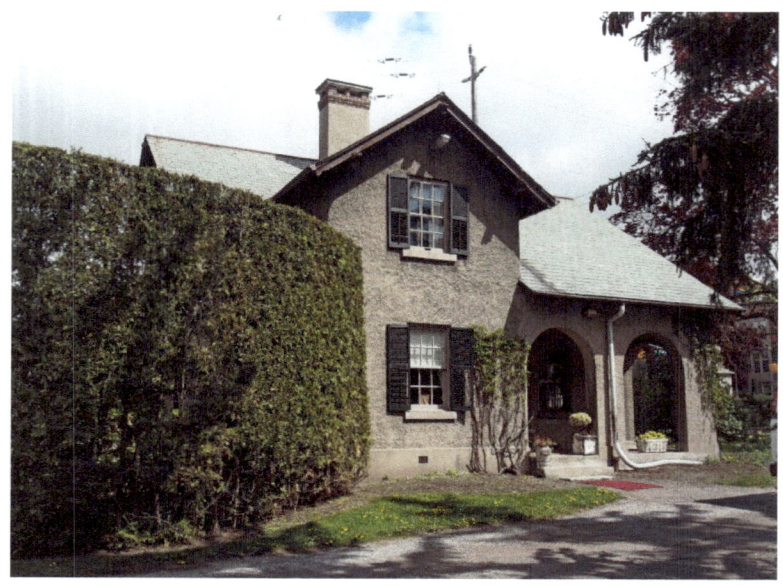

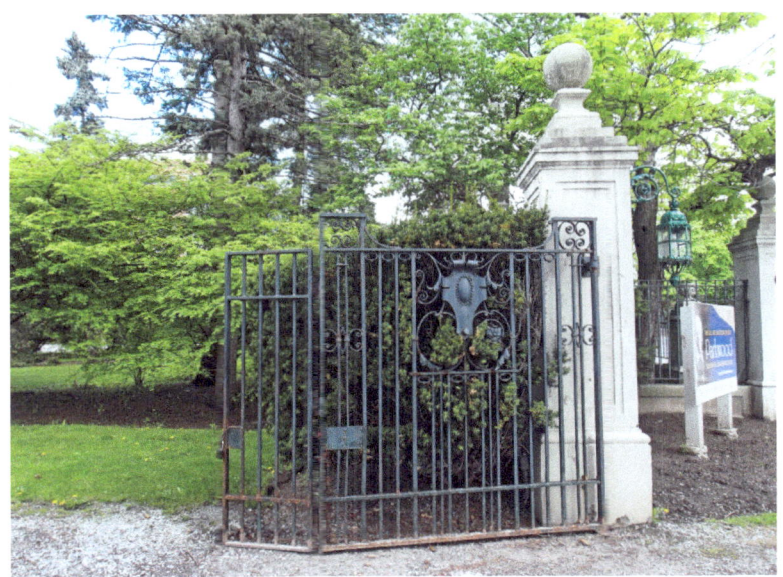

Gate to Parkwood

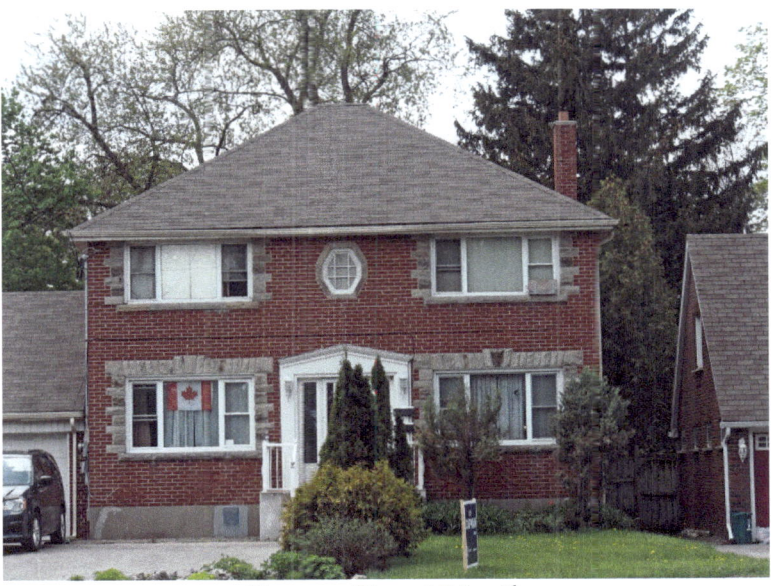

Simcoe Street North

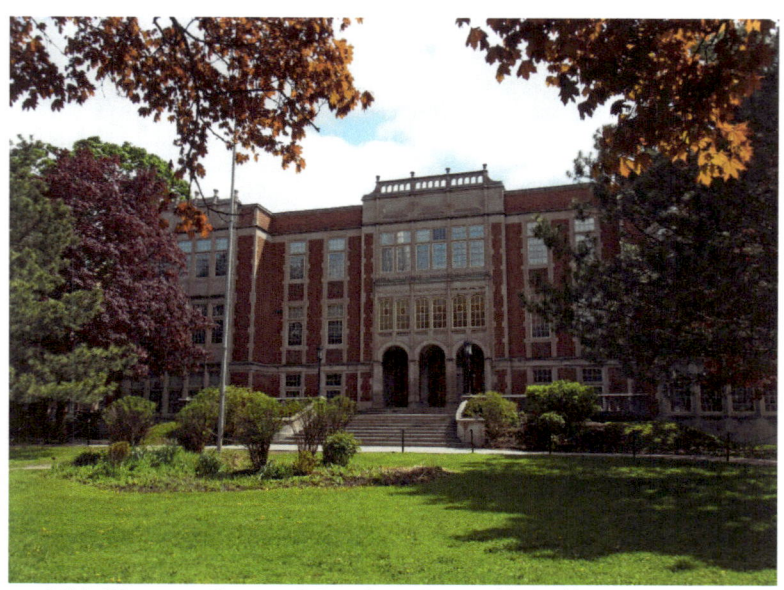

301 Simcoe Street North - O'Neill Collegiate and Vocational Institute offers a wide range of academic and extracurricular activities. It is known as an art school, drawing many students from around the Greater Toronto Area into its arts programs. The science programs are well developed, with multiple fully functional science labs.

O'Neill CVI is the oldest secondary school in Oshawa, opened in its present location in 1909. The original building is still in the core of the school, but is not visible from outside.

After several major expansions during the 1920s, OHS became Oshawa Collegiate and Vocational Institute in 1930. In the post-war era, when Oshawa began building other high schools, OCVI was renamed O'Neill Collegiate and Vocational Institute after long-time principal, Albert O'Neill, who had led its expansion and transition to collegiate status. O'Neill celebrated its 75th anniversary (as OCVI, though it is actually much older if the OHS days are included) in 2005 with a mural in the library and a reunion of students and teachers.

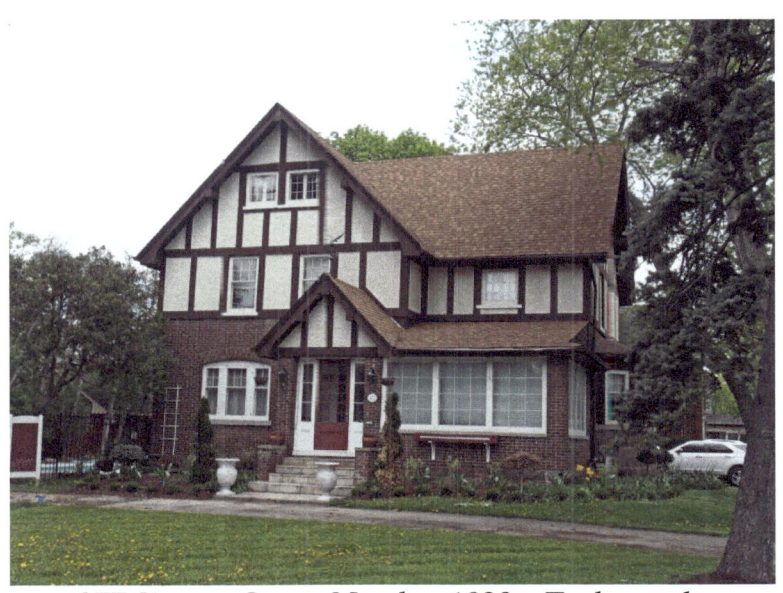

377 Simcoe Street North – 1920 – Tudor style

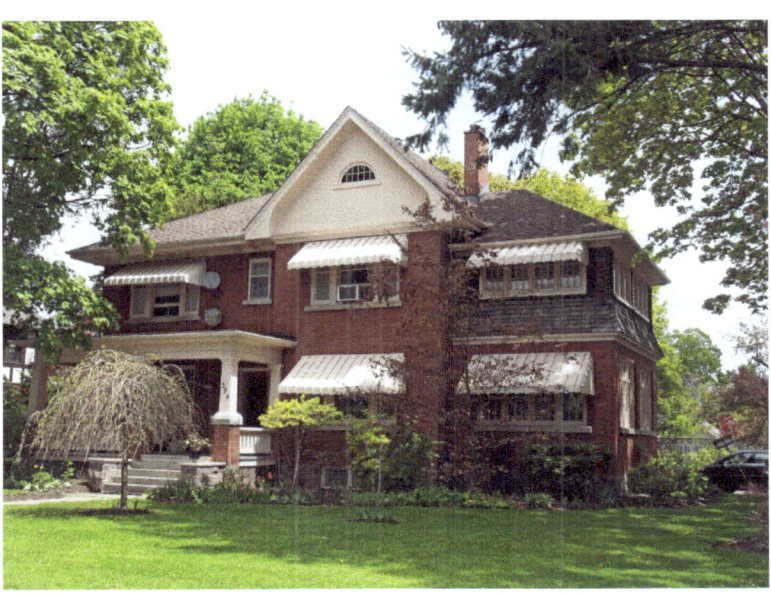

389 Simcoe Street North - 1927

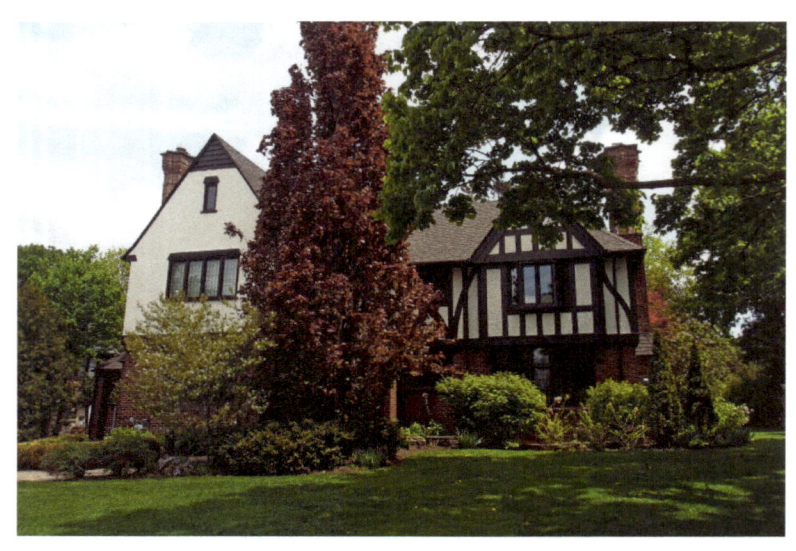

399 Simcoe Street North – 1925 – Tudor style

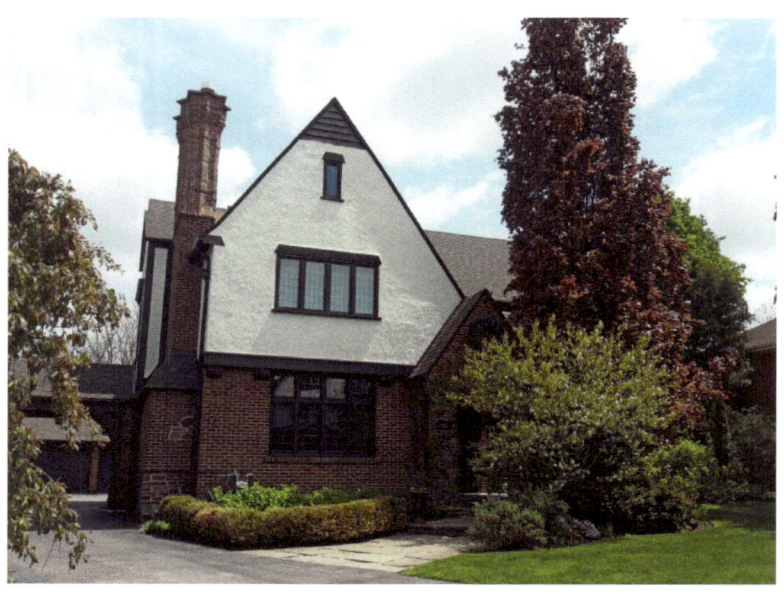

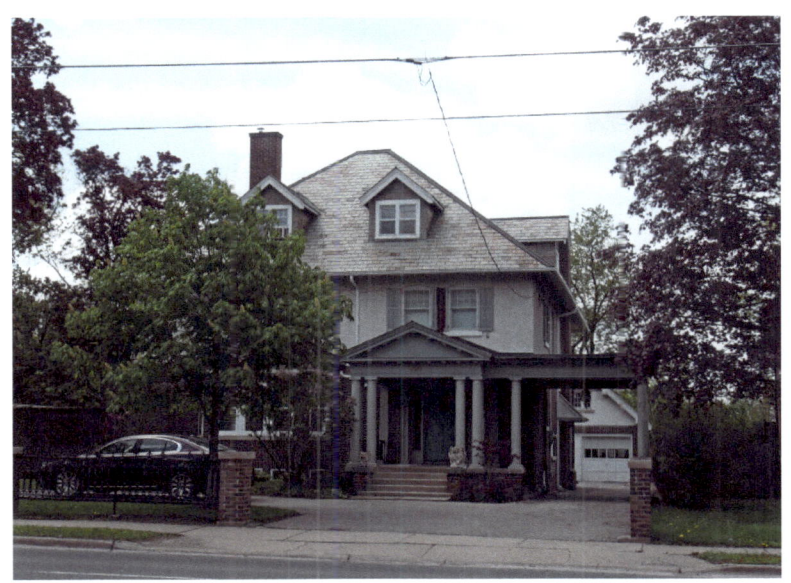

400 Simcoe Street North - 1925

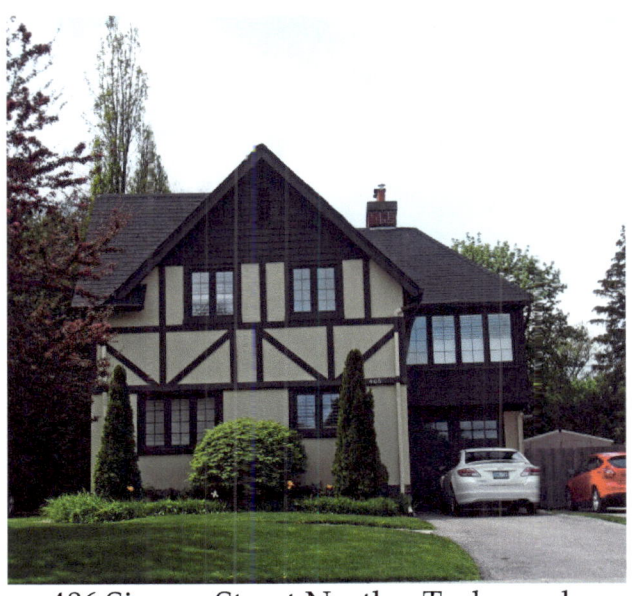

406 Simcoe Street North – Tudor style

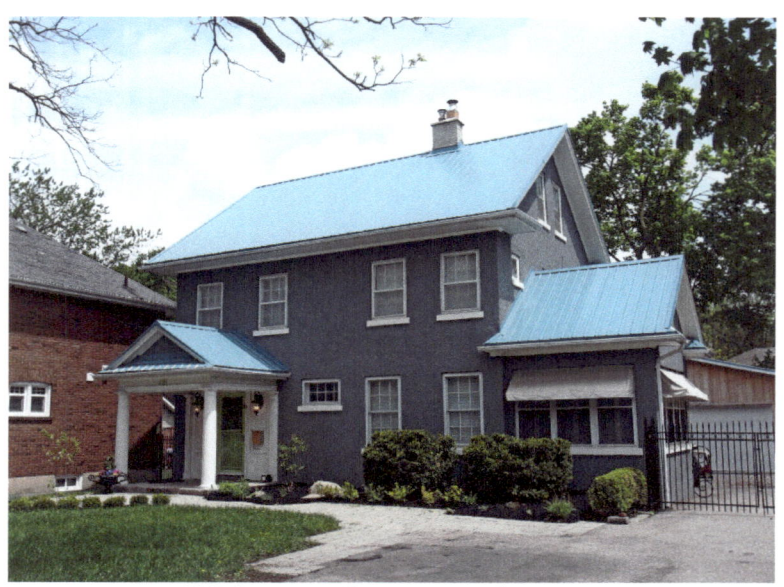

425 Simcoe Street North - 1917

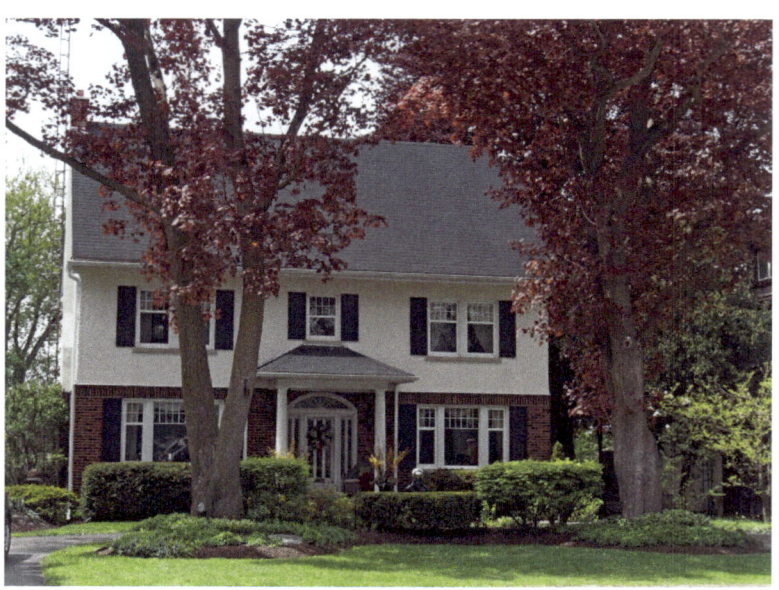

426 Simcoe Street North - 1925

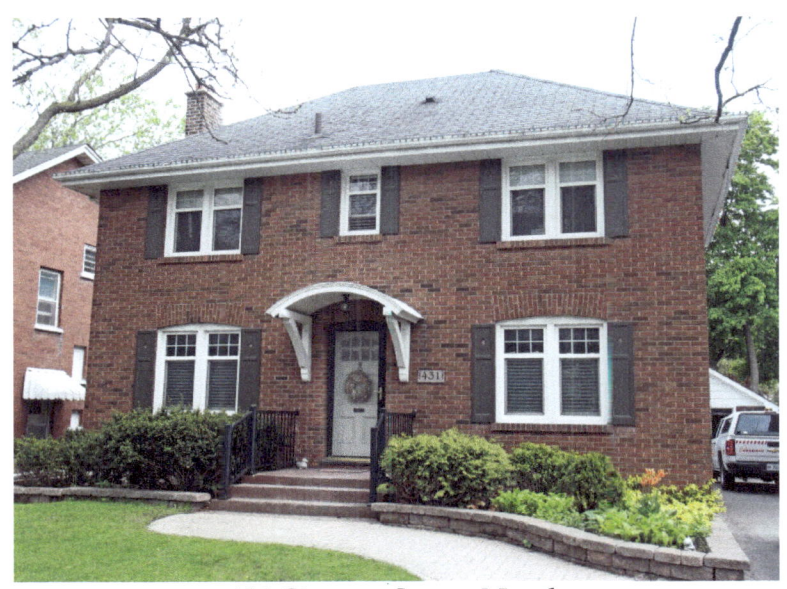

431 Simcoe Street North

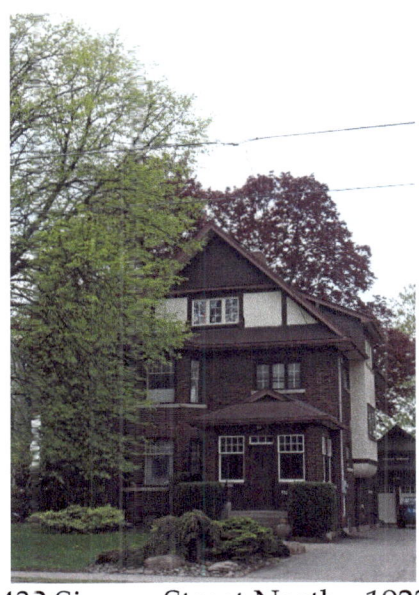

432 Simcoe Street North - 1922

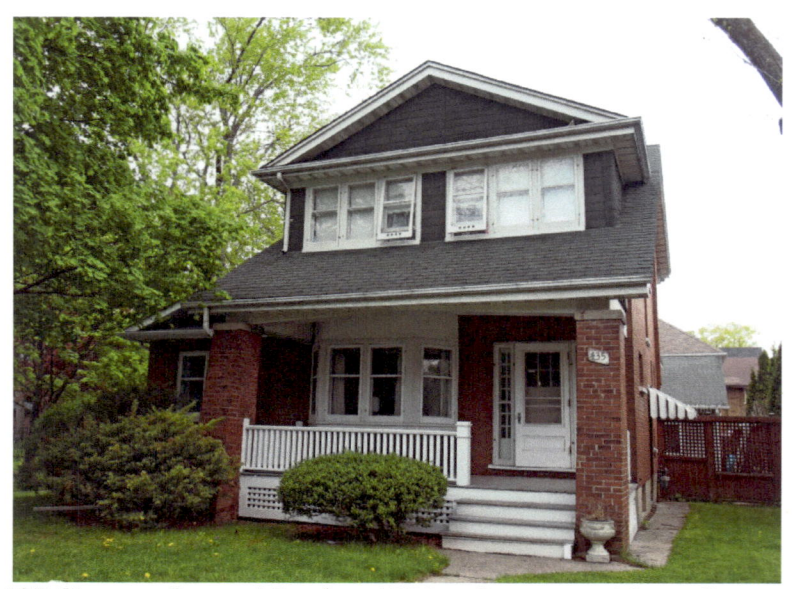

435 Simcoe Street North – 1920 – dormer with pediment

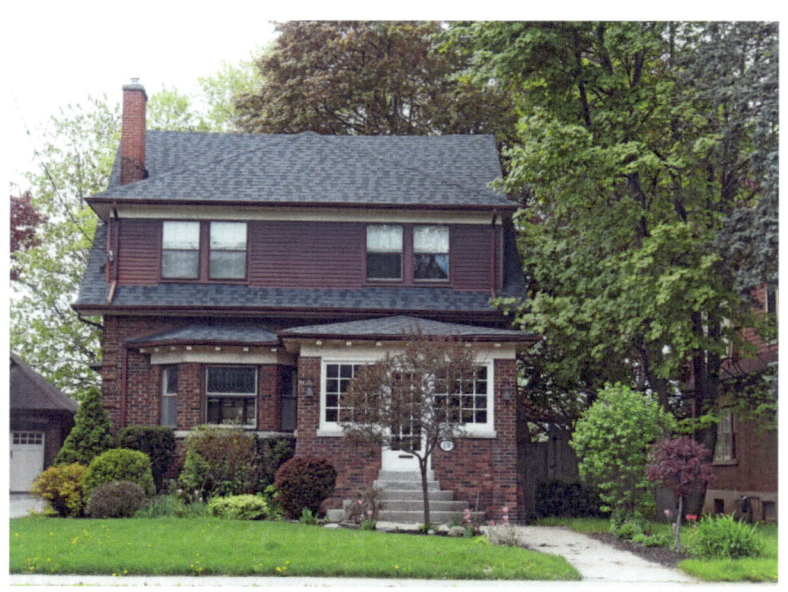

438 Simcoe Street North

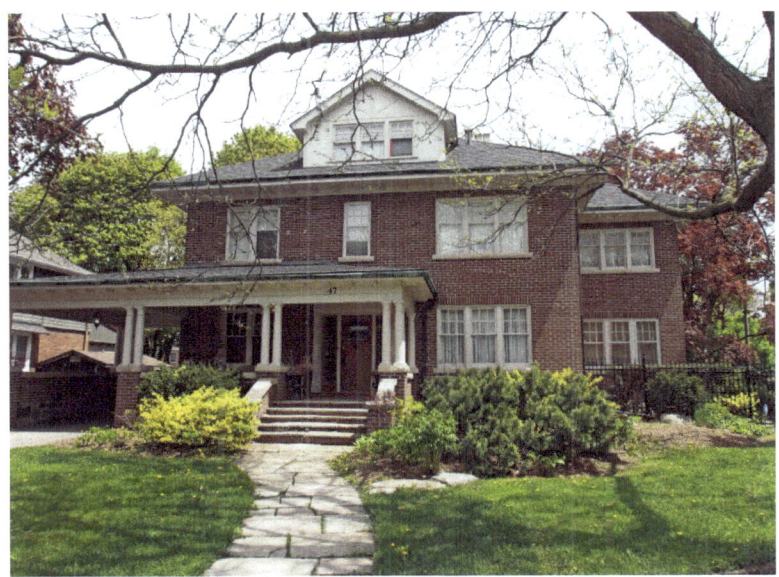

447 Simcoe Street North - 1928

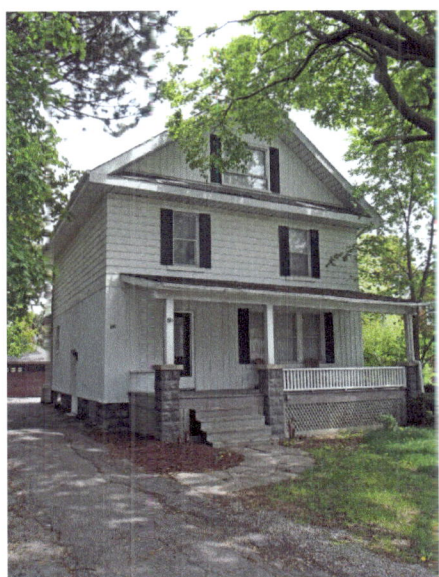

691 Simcoe Street North

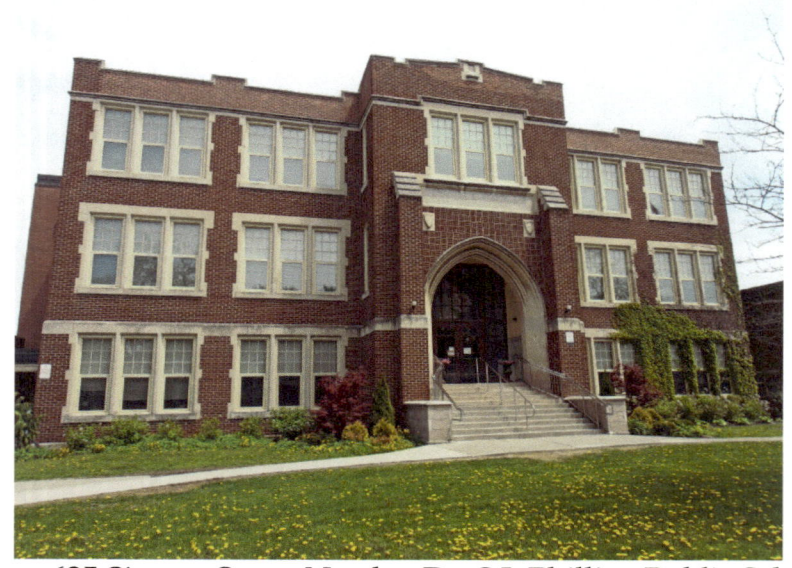

625 Simcoe Street North – Dr. S.J. Phillips Public School was originally called North Simcoe Public School and was built in 1924, the same year in which Oshawa became a city. The original three story brick building opened with a staff of eight teachers and almost 400 students. In 1952 six rooms and an auditorium were added. Another addition was added in 1956 when the student population reached 753.

In 1962 the school was renamed "Dr. SJ Phillips Public School" to show gratitude to the local dentist Dr. Stanley J. Phillips who served as a member of the Oshawa Board of Education from 1930 to 1950. Current enrollment includes students from Junior Kindergarten to Grade 8.

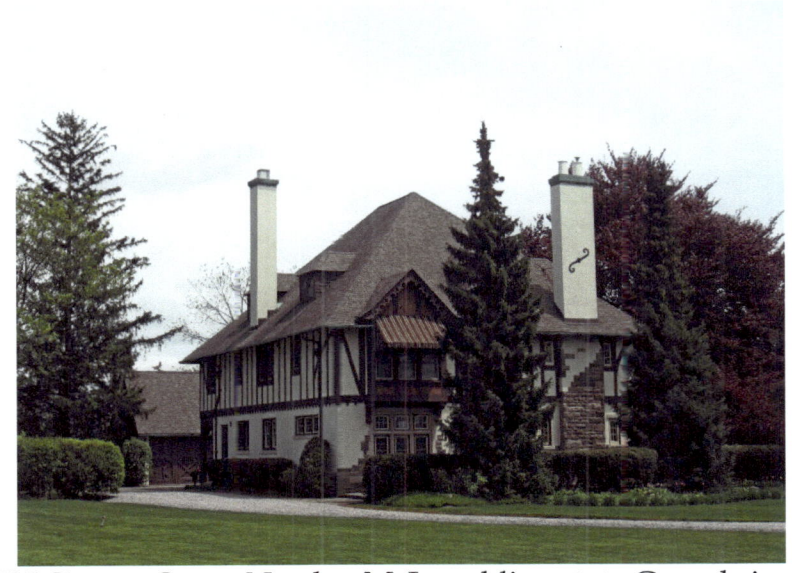

705 Simcoe Street North – McLaughlin estate Greenbriar – 1928 – Tudor style

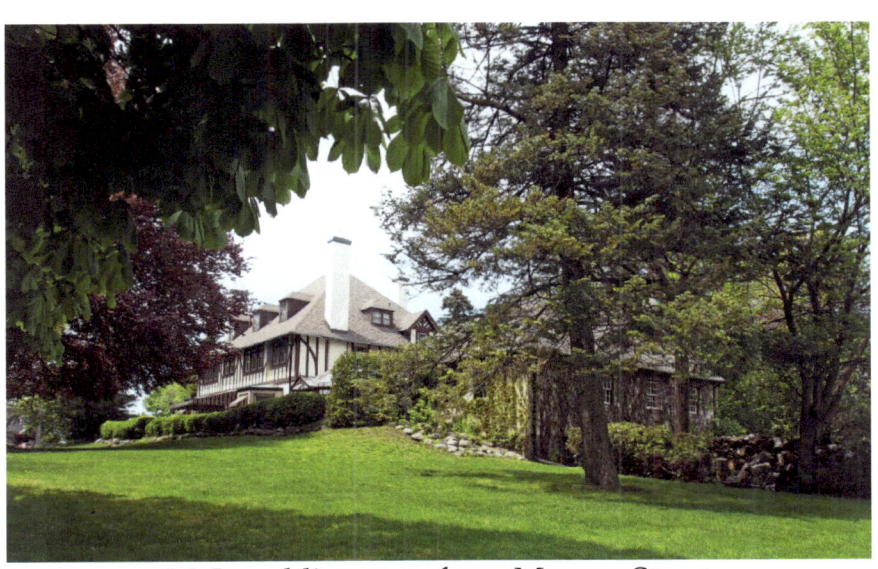

McLaughlin estate from Masson Street

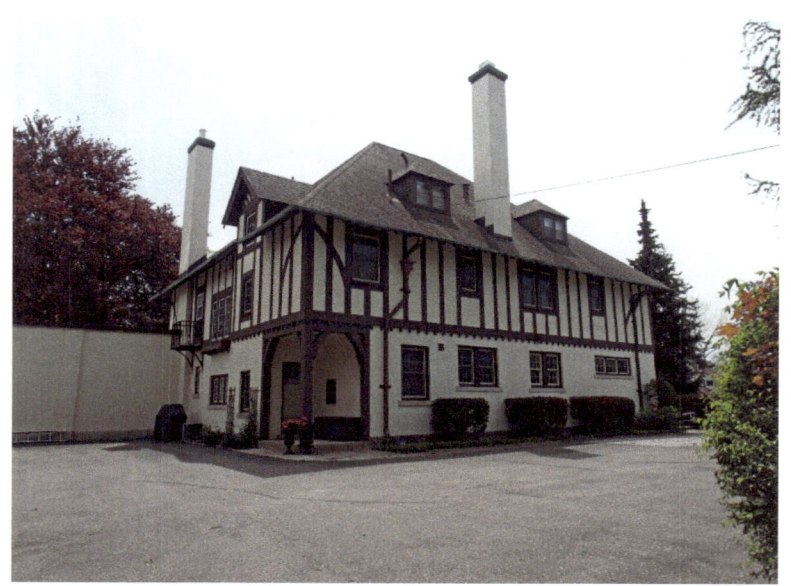
McLaughlin estate from Laracor Lane

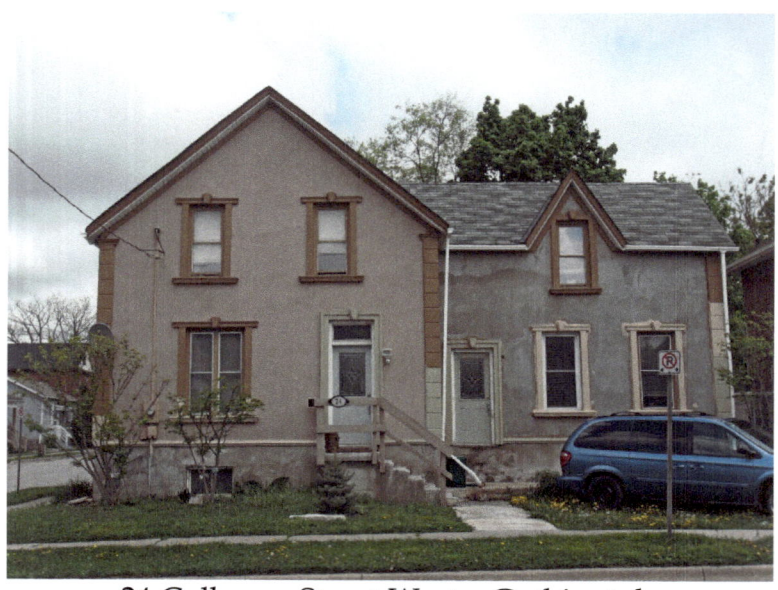
24 Colborne Street West – Gothic style

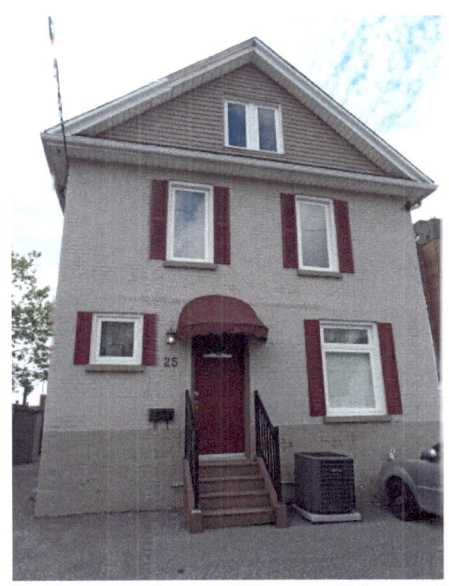

25 Colborne Street West - Edwardian

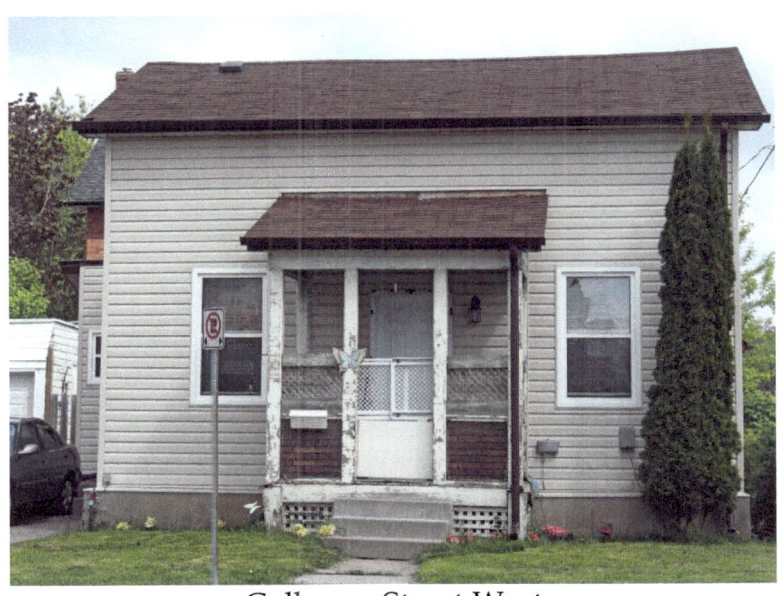

Colborne Street West

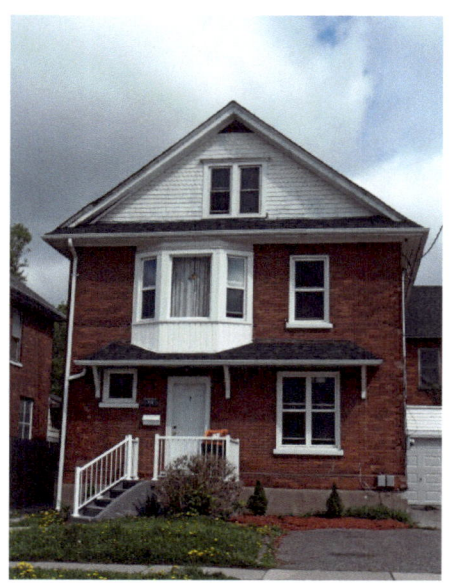

38 Colborne Street West

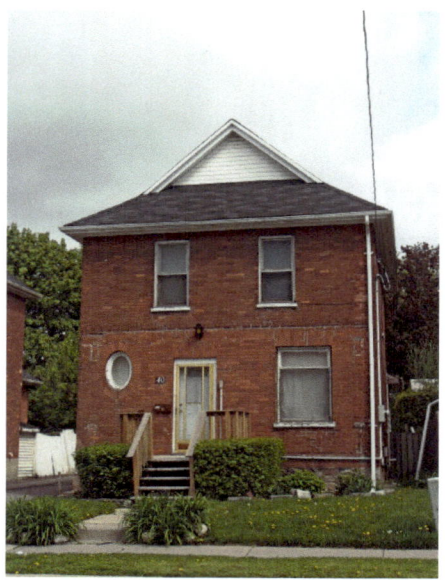

40 Colborne Street West

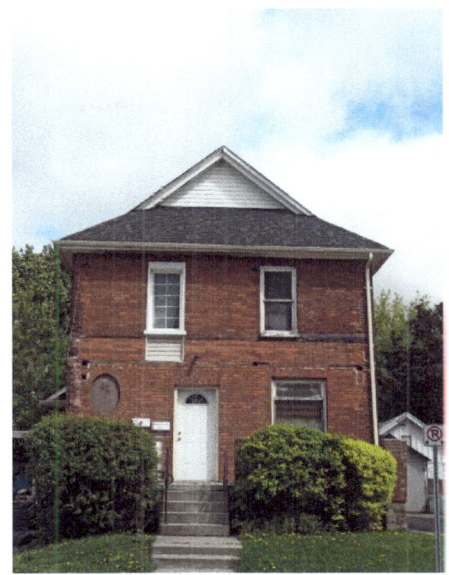

42 Colborne Street West

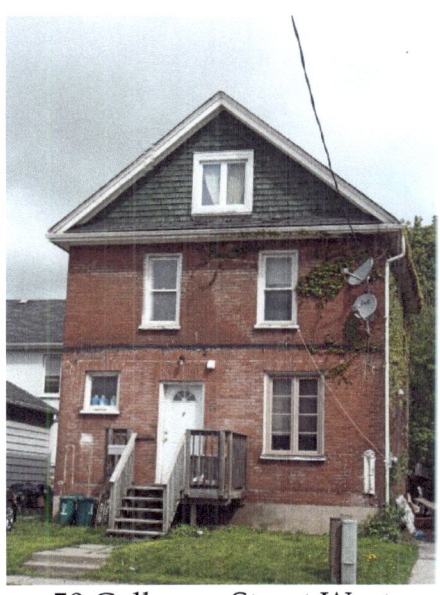

50 Colborne Street West

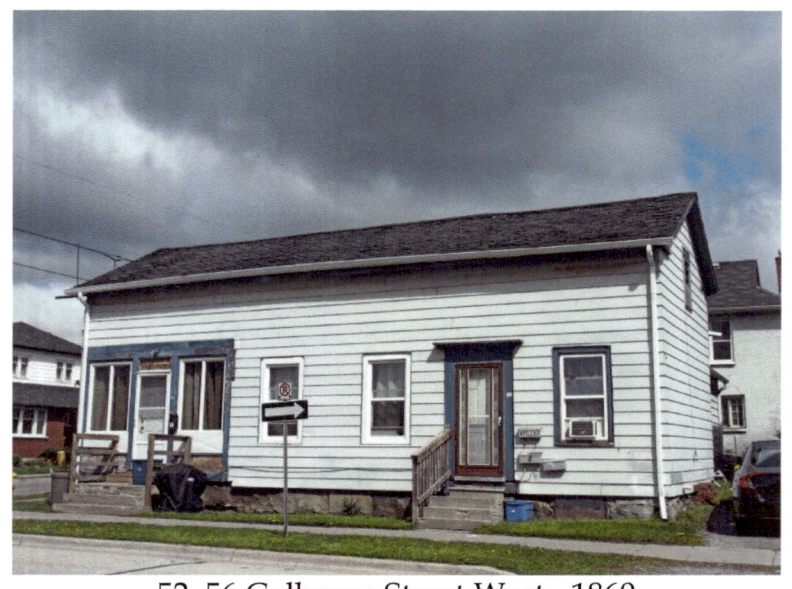

52, 56 Colborne Street West - 1860

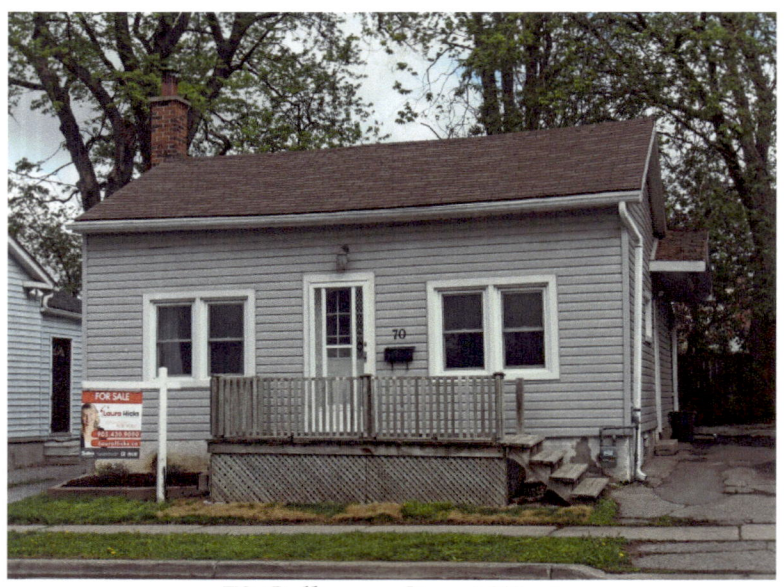

70 Colborne Street West

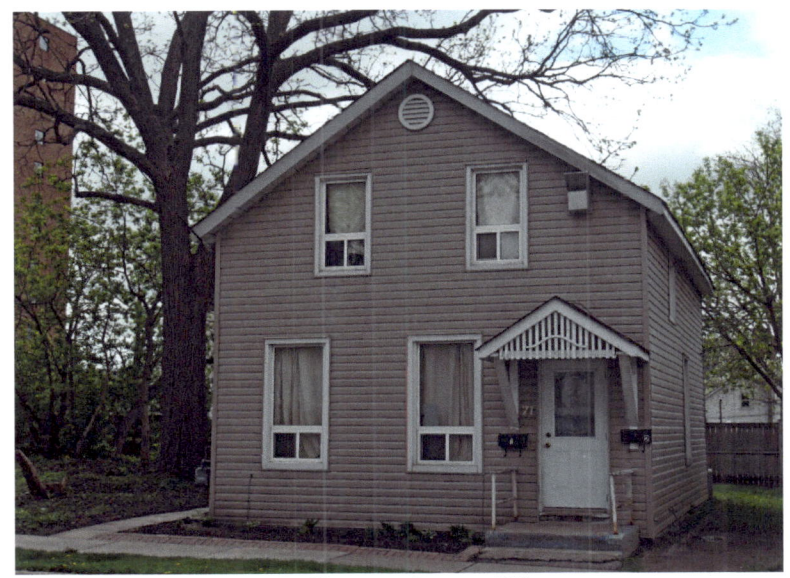

71 Colborne Street West

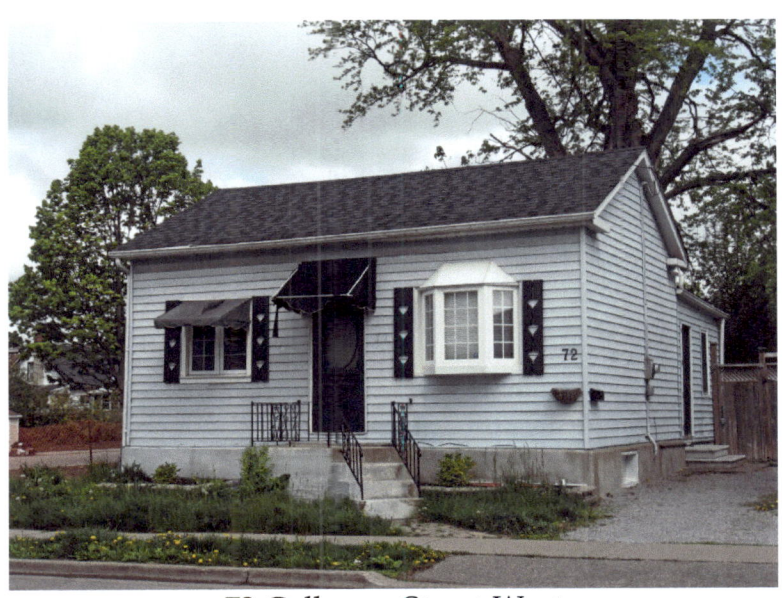

72 Colborne Street West

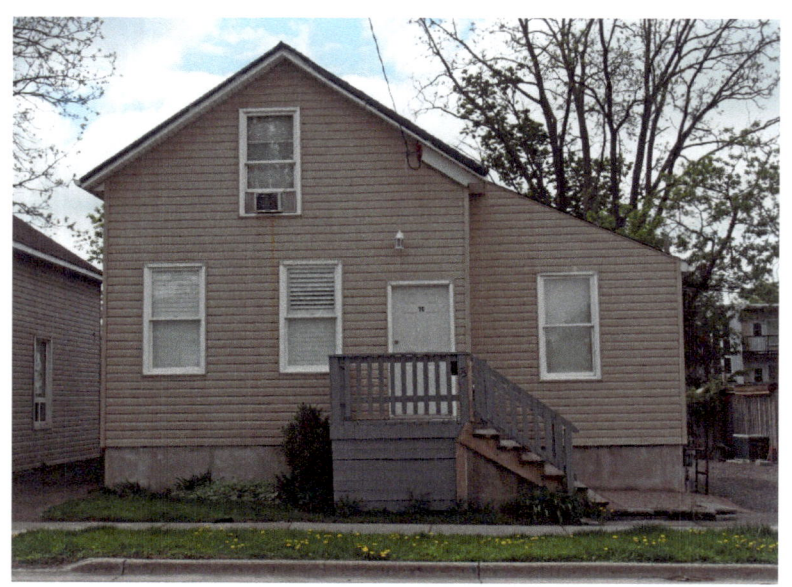

75 Colborne Street West – 1870

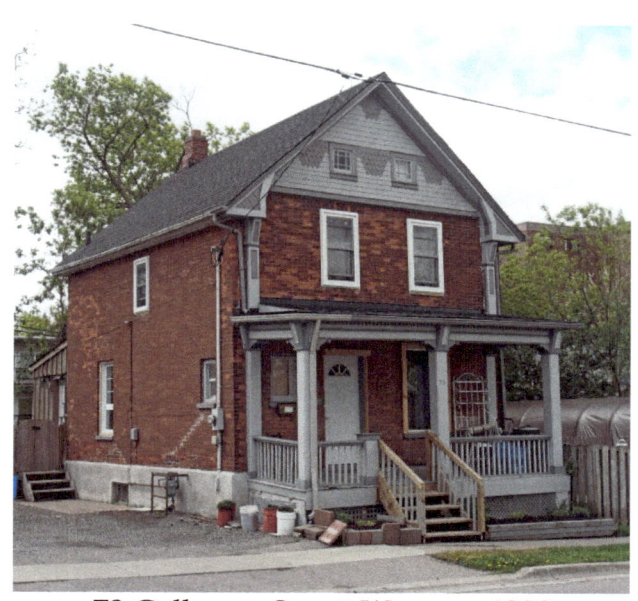

79 Colborne Street West - c. 1920

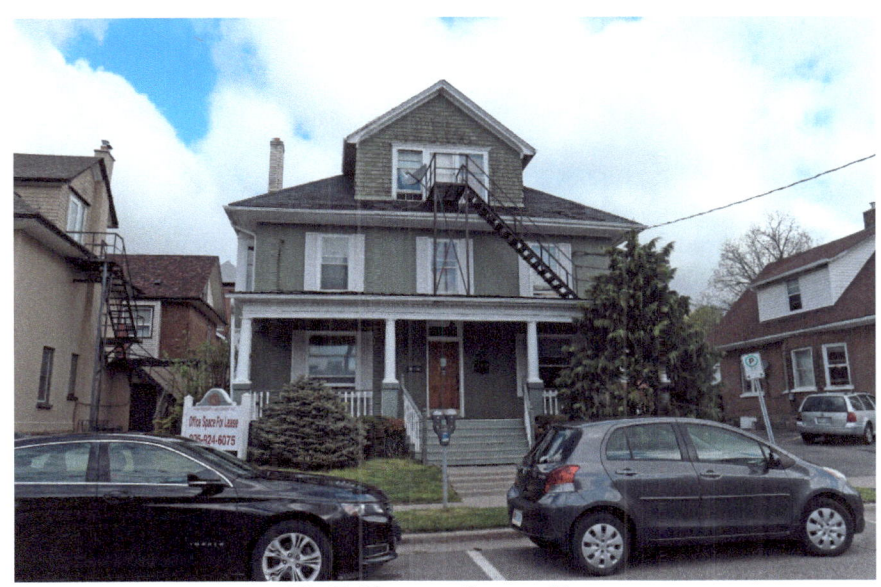

10 Colborne Street East

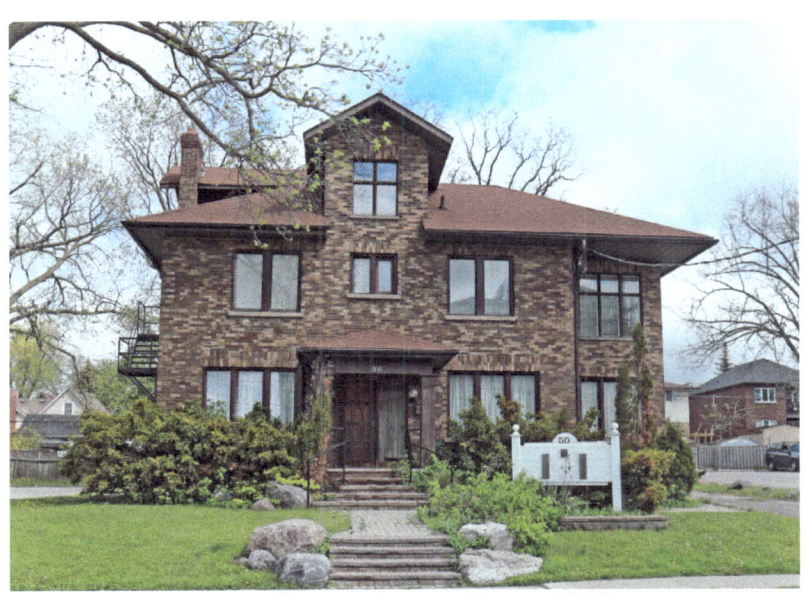

50 Colborne Street East - 1923

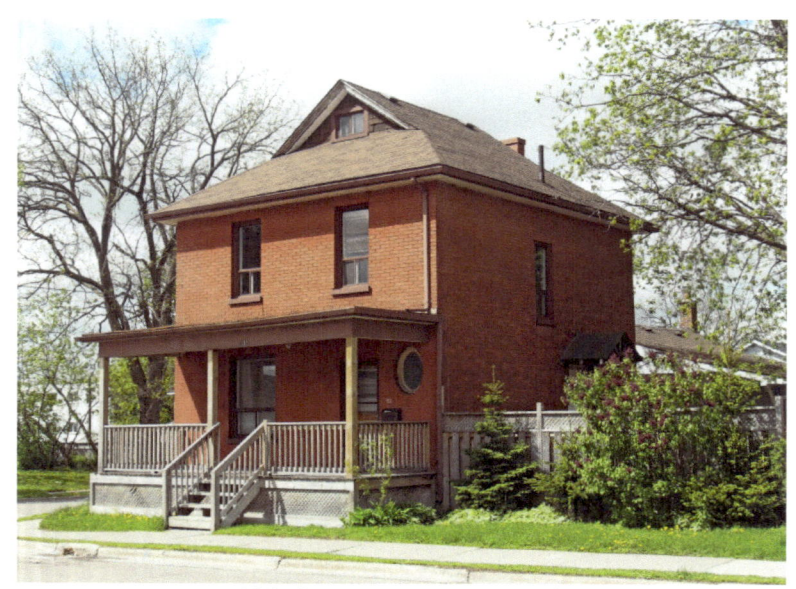

132 Centre Street North

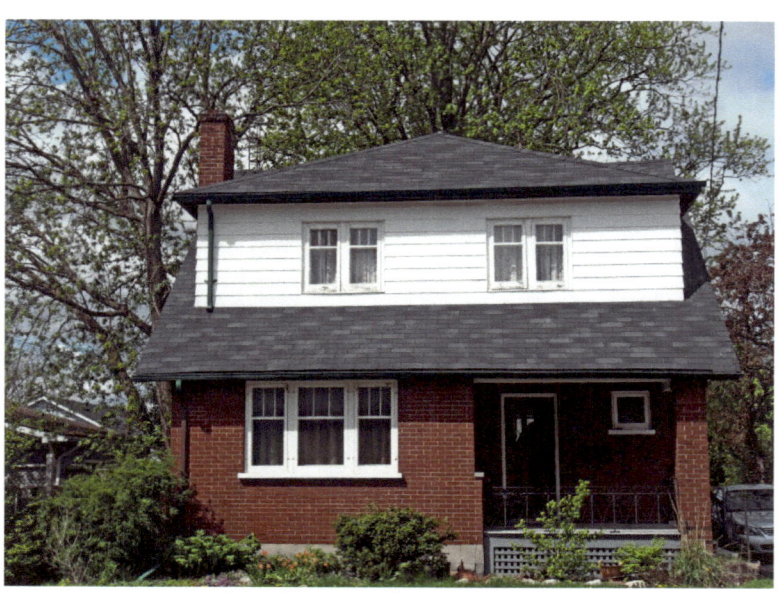

136 Centre Street North

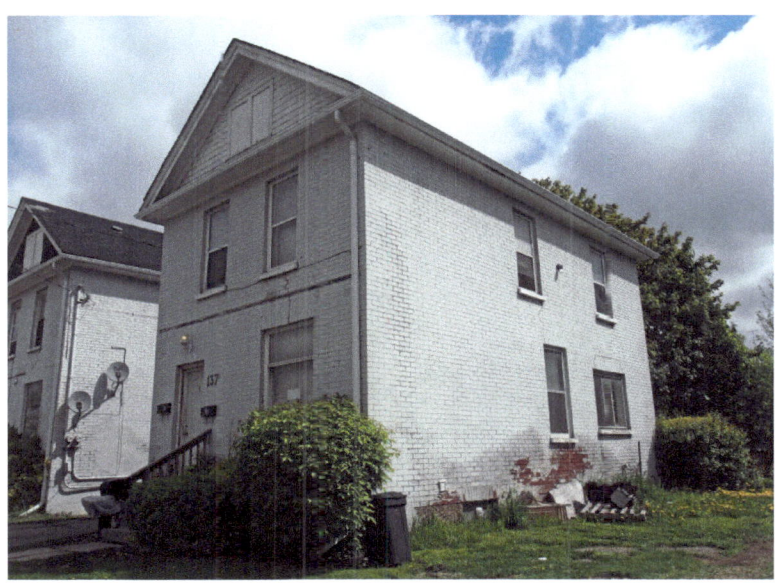

137 Centre Street North

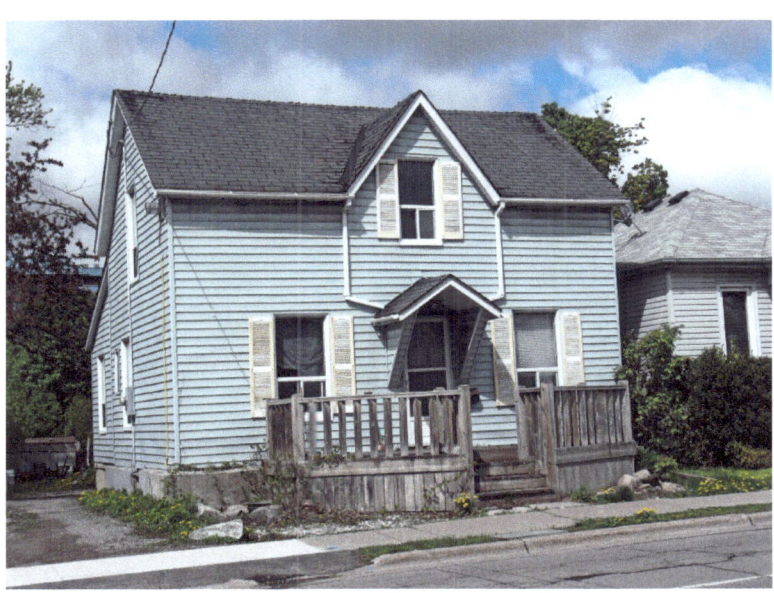

140 Centre Street North

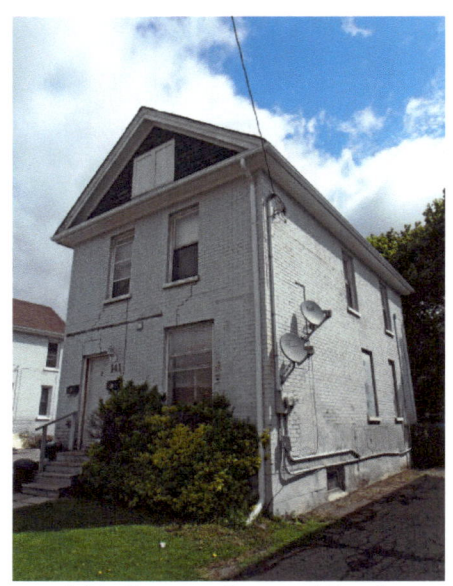

141 Centre Street North

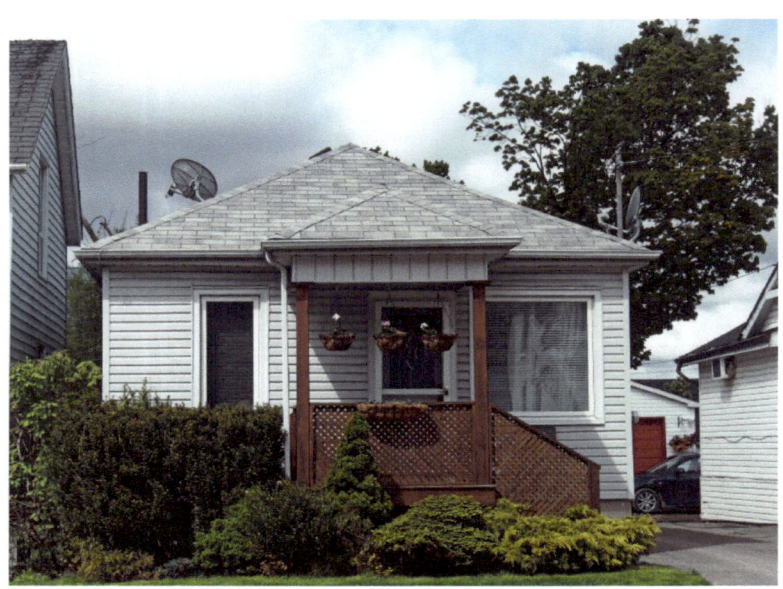

Centre Street North

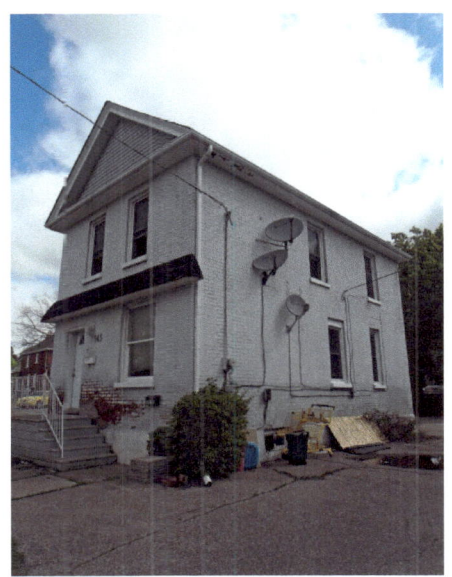

145 Centre Street North

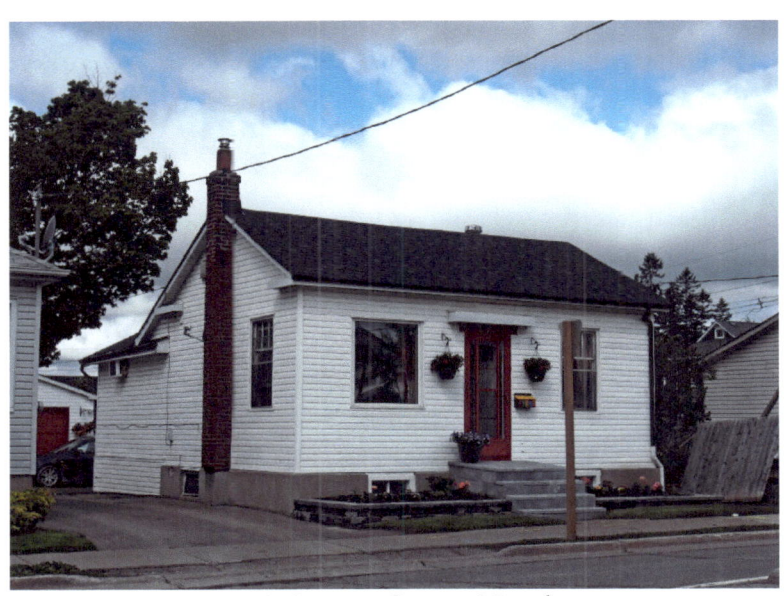

148 Centre Street North

Building Styles

Edwardian, 1900-1930 – This style bridges the ornate and elaborate styles of the Victorian era and the simplified styles of the 20th century. Edwardian Classicism provided simple, balanced facades, simple rooflines, dormer windows, large front porches, and smooth brick surfaces. Voussoirs and keystones are used sparingly and are understated. Finials and cresting are absent. Cornice brackets and braces are block-like and openings have flat arches or plain stone lintels.

Gothic Revival, 1830-1890 – These decorative buildings have sharply-pitched gables with highly detailed verge boards, pointed-arch window openings, and dichromatic brickwork. It is a common style in Ontario.

Neo-Gothic (Collegiate Gothic): is monochromatic and on a much grander scale than Gothic. Early Neo-Gothic was the decorative use of Gothic elements with a lack of knowledge and understanding of Gothic construction. Neo-Gothic tried to understand the basic principles of Gothic and used them. Early neo-Gothic churches were often plastered or painted, later neo-Gothic churches were not. An important moment in the development of neo-Gothic is the year 1853, when the hierarchy of the Roman Catholic church was fully restored in the Netherlands. Materials used were natural stone combined with brick. Around the year 1850 neo-Gothicism was maturing and increasingly became a Roman Catholic style almost exclusively. Neo-Gothic was adopted as the style for schools and universities in the early years of the 20th century. The style became so common for scholastic buildings that it is often called Collegiate Gothic. Wall buttresses and finials are added, but they are generally far too small to be of any structural benefit.

Regency Cottage, 1830-1860 – This style originated in England in 1815 and spread to Ontario later in the 19th century as British officers retired to Canada. It is a modest one-story house with a low-pitched hip roof and has a symmetrical front façade.

Tudor Revival – exposed timbers with stucco infill, multi-paned windows.

Other Books by Barbara Raue

Coins of Gold
Arrows, Indians and Love
The Life and Times of Barbara
The Cromwell Family Book
Laura Secord Discovered
Daddy Where Are You?

Montana Series
Book 1: Montana Dream
Book 2: Life on the Montana Frontier
Book 3: Montana to Boston and Back
Book 4: Montana Sons Go to War
Book 5: Montana Sons Return from War

Donaldson Series
Book 1: Rite of Passage
Book 2: Rite of Marriage

© 2021 by Barbara Raue - All the photos in this book have been taken with my cameras. I own the rights to them.

Barbara is The Authority on Saving Our History One Photo at a Time. She is pursuing her interest in photography and architecture by preserving a record through photos of old buildings from the 1800s and 1900s with their unique architecture. Enjoy the beautiful architecture in the comfort of your living room. Dream about what it was like in those by-gone days. Dream about what it was like to live in a mansion like one of those in this book.

Barbara Raue, a wife, mother and grandmother, is an avid reader and writer. She has researched and compiled several family histories. In 2010, Barbara published her book "Coins of Gold," which celebrates the courageous life of her mother, May Todd. Barbara's second book is a historical fiction "Arrows, Indians and Love" which takes place in Boonesborough, Kentucky during the time of Daniel Boone. In 2013, Barbara published *The Cromwell Family Book* in which she traces her ancestry generations back into Great Britain. Her second novel is called *Laura Secord Discovered,* in which the story of Laura's service during the War of 1812 is shared. Barbara's memoir is titled *Daddy Where Are You?* It tells of her life growing up without a father. Five novels in the Montana Series have been published, *Montana Dream*, *Life on the Montana Frontier*, *Montana to Boston and Back*, *Montana Sons Go to War*, and *Montana Sons Return from War*. The Donaldson series of two novels is available: *Rite of Passage* and *Rite of Marriage*.

This is a link to Barbara's website to view all of her books
http://barbararaue.ca

www.ingramcontent.com/pod-product-compliance
Lightning Source LLC
Chambersburg PA
CBHW040243220526
45473CB00001B/356